ARE YOU ROBBING GOD?

TITHING PRINCIPLE: THE KEY TO HEALING, RESTORATION AND ABUNDANCE.

THIERRY D. OSUNGU

Thierry D. Osungu
Are Your Robbing God?

Published by Spines
ISBN: 979-8-89383-399-7

DEDICATION

To the One I call "Father", whom the body of Christ knows as the Alpha and the Omega, the Beginning and the End, The Author and the Finisher of our faith – this humble offering is dedicated with profound gratitude, unwavering devotion, and unbridled love.

In the sacred journey of penning these words for years, I finally made it, and I am acutely aware of the divine inspiration that has guided my hand and illuminated my heart. To our Lord and Savior, Jesus Christ, who has been the beacon in the darkest nights and the steady hand in turbulent seas, this book is dedicated.

May the words within these pages be a fragrant offering, a melody of praise, and a testament to the boundless grace that has been poured upon me. To the Almighty God, whose has been the beacon in the darkest nights and steady hand in turbulent seas, this book is dedicated.

May the words within these pages be a fragrant offering, a melody of praise, and a testament to the boundless grace that has been poured upon me. To the Almighty, whose mercy knows no end, and whose love knows no bounds, I dedicated this works as an act of worship.

To my family and friends, the God's fearing people who have walked beside me through valleys and mountain peaks, your unwavering support and encouragement have reflected God's love in my life. This book is dedicated to you, with heartfelt appreciation for the warmth of your presence and strength of your prayers.

To the readers who embark on this literary pilgrimage, may these pages be a source of inspiration and not of judgment, reflection and not of guilt, and transformation and not of stagnation. As you delve into the narrative woven with threads of faith, hope, and love, may you feel the gentle whisper of the holy Spirit, drawing you close to the heart of God.

In dedicating this book to the Divine Trinity – Father, Son, and Holy Spirit _ I acknowledge that without Him, this endeavour would be futile. It is my prayer that every word written in this book serves as an instrument of His peace, a vessel of His truth, and proclamation of His love.

With profound gratitude and open heart, I dedicate this Christian book to the one who authored my life and continues to author my story – the God of grace the Redeemer of souls, and my one and only Everlasting Father.

CONTENTS

ACKNOWLEDGMENTS

As I embark on this new, incredible, inspired, and committed literacy journey, I find myself overwhelmed with gratitude and joy. *Are You Robbing God? Tithing Principle The Key to Healing, Restoration and Abundance* is more than just a book; it is a tapestry woven with threads of knowledge, experiences, and testimonies.

I want to take a moment to give all glory and honor to the Eternal God Almighty, through my Savior and Lord, Jesus Christ. He is the One who placed this project in my heart and has continuously guided me toward a deeper understanding of the balance between theology and the spiritual aspects of tithing. He allowed His servants to minister to me during my journey, enabling me to reach where I am today. Ministers such as Pastor Anthony Ramsey and his wife, Pastor Marvella Ramsey from Kingdom Living Church in Flint, Michigan, have played a significant role in my life. I hold Pastor Ramsey in the highest regard as a great man of God. God placed him in my path to teach me about giving, the importance of giving as a Christian, and the spiritual impact it has on one's life. I joined Kingdom Living Church in the summer of 2010 after moving to Flint, Michigan in late 2009. Pastor Ramsey has a tradition of dedicating five minutes every Sunday to teach about giving before starting his sermons. These short but profound messages resonated with me and planted seeds of understanding in fertile ground. Through these five-minute sermons, I continued to learn more about giving until I became a devoted giver.

Pastor Patrick Mubobo from Change the Nations Church (CTNC) also deserves my gratitude for his love, teachings, and ongoing prayers for me and my family. I believe that many of his prayers for my family and me have been answered because the grace of God is upon us every day. Lastly, I want to express my heartfelt thanks to all those who have made this journey possible.

To the Readers

To all of you who have chosen this book, allowed its words to dance in your minds, and embraced the stories within, thank you for giving life to our words. Your curiosity, open hearts, and willingness to embark on this literary adventure mean more to me than words can express.

Family and Friends

To the pillars of support in my life, my family and friends, I want to express my sincere gratitude for your unwavering encouragement. Your belief in our vision has been the anchor that has propelled me through the highs and lows of the creative process. I am especially grateful to my mother, Rehema P. Mangaza, for her unconditional love and support for my siblings and me. As a single mother, she has shown me the utmost respect for women from all walks of life. Her resilience and countless sacrifices have paved the way for a better life for my brother, sister, and me. Whenever I see a single mother tirelessly juggling multiple jobs, working overtime, or pursuing an education while raising children alone, I am reminded of my mother and see her strength in them. I cannot help but admire them, and for that, I say, thank you, Mother, for everything and your compassion toward others.

I also express my heartfelt appreciation to my brother, Guy Osungu, and his wife, Nadine Berodes, as well as my sisters, Sheila Libali and Kelly McCollough. Their love and unwavering support have always been there for me in times of need.

Lastly, I want to convey my deepest gratitude to my wife, Carine I. Osungu. She has been my powerhouse for me and our children. She is my rock, and a friend I can truly trust. She holds my heart and has also been instrumental in my decision to become a faithful tither and giver, inspired by the message of giving from our faith leaders in Jesus Christ. She is a woman of unwavering faith, who loves God through Christ Jesus. Her prayers have been a guiding force, speaking to me, inspiring me, and teaching me the path of a Christian. Because she heeded God's voice, we have been able to withstand and overcome numerous challenges, including economic crises that have affected many others.

To all of you, I want to emphasize that this book is not just mine, but also yours. It is a testament to the love, support, and belief that you have all showered upon me.

Editors and publishing team

A special acknowledgment goes out to the unsung heroes behind the scenes—our dedicated editors at Sermon-Assist, book design team at HmdPublishing and publishing team. Your keen eyes, constructive feedback, and invaluable insights have transformed this into its best possible version. As passionate individuals, thank you for believing in this story and working tirelessly to bring it to the shelves. Your dedication has been the wind beneath my wings. From the cover design to the meticulous editing, your attention to detail has made this book a visual and literary masterpiece. I am deeply grateful for your time, expertise, and commitment.

Faithful Tithers

To the faithful tithers who have graciously agreed to share their testimonies in this book, we extend our heartfelt gratitude. Your testimonies have not only imparted knowledge but also inspired us and deepened our understanding of tithing through your individual experiences. Your storytelling has been intricately woven into the very fabric of these chapters. This book serves as a powerful testament to the lessons we have learned from the word of God. As Revelation 12:11 states, "And they overcame him by the blood of the Lamb, and by the word of their testimony; and they loved not their lives unto the death."

Lastly, we would like to express our gratitude to everyone who has been a part of this collective journey – through the highs and lows, the tears and laughter.

As we release this creation into the world, we do so with immense gratitude and humility. May these pages of tithing resonate with your own testimonies as faithful givers and touch the hearts of my fellow Christians who may be encountering this principle for the first time or seeking a deeper understanding of it.

With love and appreciation,

Your beloved brother in Christ, Thierry D. Osungu

PREFACE

Tithing is a controversial subject within the body of Christ. While I would like to believe that most Christians agree that it is biblical to pay tithes, others view it as an ancient ritual. Some Christians fear that committing to tithing may lead to giving out of guilt, rather than true conviction, and there are even those who do not believe it is biblical at all. This is where the problem lies, and division begins.

This book on tithing is a humble attempt to explore the profound teaching embedded within the pages of the Bible. It aims to show that tithing is not merely a transaction, but a sacred act of worship. It is a symphony that harmonizes the human heart with its creator, the Eternal God.

As we embark on this journey through the verses that speak to the origin and essence of tithing, let us remember that tithing is not confined to the material realm alone. It is a spiritual practice that transcends possessions and wealth, reaching into the depths of our souls. The testimonies and lessons contained in this book are not meant to prescribe guilt or obligation, but rather to serve as guideposts pointing toward the boundless joy that springs forth when we give with open hearts.

The Bible simplifies this topic through parables and teachings that weave a narrative illuminating the transformative power of tithing. It is a theme that resonates across time, reminding us that in tithing, we align ourselves with God's everlasting blessings that flow through the very fabric of creation. Through reflections on biblical verses and stories, the aim is not to dictate a specific method of tithing but to inspire thoughtful and purposeful engagement with the resources entrusted to us.

As for us in the body of Christ, we recognize that the call to pay tithes takes on different forms. Each act of tithing contributes to the greater symphony of love and faith toward our Creator, God Almighty, as revealed to us in Scripture. As we take you on this journey of exploring tithing by presenting verses and insights within these pages, let us do so with open hearts and minds. Recognize that the act of tithing is a reciprocal dance in the spiritual realm, blessing all parties involved and beyond. May this exploration foster a deeper understanding of the sacred nature of generosity and inspire a more profound commitment to embodying its principles in our daily lives.

May this book be a source of inspiration, a guide for reflection, and a catalyst for transformative action as we navigate the path of tithing in accordance with the timeless wisdom of Scripture.

With gratitude and reverence,

Thierry D. Osungu, Author

CHAPTER 1

RETURN TO ME AND I WILL RETURN TO YOU!

*I the Lord do not change. So you, the descendants of Jacob, are not destroyed. **7 Ever since the time of your ancestors you have turned away from my decrees and have not kept them.** Return to me, and I will return to you," says the Lord Almighty. "But you ask, 'How are we to return?'8 "Will a mere mortal rob God? Yet you rob me. "But you ask, 'How are we robbing you?'"In tithes and offerings. 9 You are under a curse—your whole nation—because you are robbing me. 10 Bring the whole tithe into the storehouse, that there may be food in my house. **Test me in this**," says the Lord Almighty, "and see if I will not throw open the floodgates of heaven and pour out so much blessing that there will not be room enough to store it. 11 I will prevent pests from devouring your crops, and the vines in your fields will not drop their fruit before it is ripe," says the Lord Almighty. 12 "Then all the nations will call you blessed, for yours will be a delightful land," says the Lord Almighty. (Malachi 3:6-12, emphasis mine)*

Malachi Chapter 3 draws attention to the significance of honoring God through tithes and offerings and emphasizes the spiritual influence that tithing and offering can have on our lives. This chapter serves as the focal point for understanding the principle of tithing and its impact on our spiritual, emotional, and physical well-being.

According to God, when we fail to pay our tithes and offerings, we are robbing Him and consequently subjecting ourselves to a financial curse. This curse extends to the entire nation if Christians are robbing God, to the individual homes if any of "the saved ones" are guilty, and to the church if any of "the believers" are robbing God. Are you living from paycheck to paycheck? Do you want your home to be under a financial curse for stealing a few dollars from God? Have you ever heard someone say, "Every time I have money in my hands, it just disappears, and sometimes I don't even know where it went"? Are you that person? If so, God is speaking to you.

Let me be clear: this book is not about making you feel guilty or convincing you to give out of guilt. My intention is not to coerce you into tithing, just as God did not intend it when He mentioned it in Malachi Chapter 3.

God began the Old Testament by providing everything and abundantly blessing humankind. However, He closed the Old Testament by exposing the fraudulent ways of humanity. Since the fall, God has been seeking for us to fully reconnect with Him, to understand that as citizens of His kingdom, we need to put Him before anything else. That is why the greatest commandment God gave us is, "Love your God with all your heart, all your soul, and with all your might" (Deuteronomy 6:5).

Giving is an expression of your heart. This is evident when the young man approached Jesus, boasting about how well he obeyed all the Ten Commandments. Jesus instructs him to give everything he has to the poor. The young man walks away sad because he sought self-righteousness. What he didn't realize is that by not being willing to give "with all his heart," he was already violating the greatest commandment and all the others. By obeying Jesus and being willing to give his wealth to the poor, he would have proven that he truly obeyed and fulfilled all the commandments.

When you violate one commandment, you violate them all. Hence, I emphasized that it's not about making you feel guilty or asking you to give out of guilt, but rather, it's about fulfilling a relationship and worshiping God. This is the only time we can test God because He told us to do so.

I used to rob God with every paycheck and all my earnings. Tithing was part of my monthly budget, but not the most important part. Every time I got paid, I barely had enough money to cover my bills, leaving me with nothing left. The money would disappear before I could even count to five. I would go back to work as soon as I ran out of money, putting in extra hours to make more just to afford the endless bills. It was a vicious cycle that seemed impossible to escape.

God says that lack is a curse. He hates poverty and doesn't want us to be poor. That's why He placed the first man amidst abundance. Part of our poverty is our own doing. We don't trust God, and we rob Him whenever the opportunity arises. Living in lack is not how we should live in our households or even in our nations. How can we transition from living in lack to experiencing abundance in our households and communities? As believers, we need to pause and decide to bring the whole tithe into the storehouse. We shouldn't tithe occasionally or from time to time. We must do it all the time. This includes tithing from our wages, side jobs, passive income, residuals, royalties, or any other income sources we tap into, as well as when someone blesses us financially. So, repeat after me: "From now on, I will bring the whole tithe into the storehouse."

What Is a Store House?

The storehouse, in this context, refers to your local church or temple as stated in Malachi 3:10. It is important to note that the local church is not only a storehouse but also a treasure house. The French version of the Bible translates the word "storehouse" as "treasure house." In this house, there should be no lack, as it is a place of abundance. God refers to the church as a house of treasure, symbolizing its connection to the kingdom of God, which is the primary treasure house. When you bring your tithes and offerings to the local church, you are contributing to the kingdom of God. As a result, the abundance in God's treasure house will replenish your own treasure house on Earth. According to Deuteronomy 28:8, you also have a storehouse, and the Lord will bless you in it and all your endeavors. These three storehouses are interconnected (Malachi 3:10).

(See figure 1 below.)

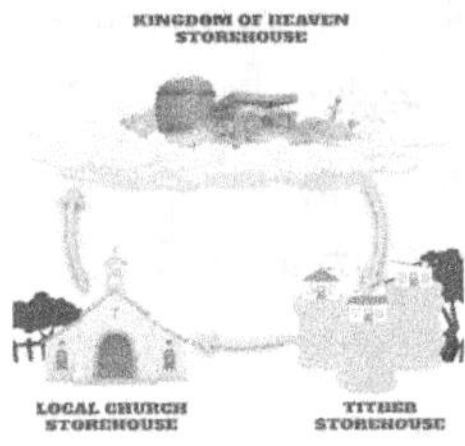

Figure 1: Storehouse + Storehouse + Storehouse = Abundance (Zero Lack)

It really is that simple. You can't deny that you want to take God at His word and test Him on this principle, just as He instructed you. Since you believe that Malachi Chapter 3 is not outdated, God has Made It Simple and Spiritual (MISS) for us. Test me. Give and receive. By doing so, you can observe God's hand in action. If you don't follow the principle illustrated in Figure 1, you will be a part of the group of people in Figure 2 below. This illustrates a state of lack.

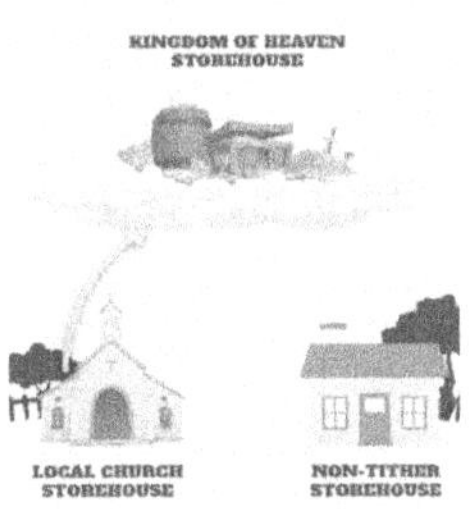

What is the difference between figure one and figure two? In Figure 1, you apply the principle in your storehouse by initiating a connection with your tithes. These tithes are then brought to the storehouse on Earth, which we have identified as the local church and is part of the kingdom of God. Through this connection, all three storehouses operate seamlessly together. However, in Figure 2, the principle is not applied. The local church stays connected to the kingdom of heaven's storehouse, but your storehouse is disconnected; therefore, you have an empty storehouse. In a time of need, the house in Figure 2 will experience a lack.

It is important to note that you are the one who initiates this connection, and as a result, the provision you pour into the storehouse comes back to you abundantly. Let's take John Doe as an example. John earns an income of $1,000, and he sets aside 10 percent ($100) of his earnings as tithes, which he brings to his local church. This 10 percent connects John's storehouse to the kingdom of God's storehouse. In the heavenly places, this action alerts God that John has taken on His challenge. From His mighty throne, God gives the order to release abundant provision into John's storehouse. At an expected or unexpected moment, John realizes that his storehouse has been abundantly replenished, not just by one-fold, but by hundreds of folds. This process truly works, for God does not lie.

Brother John Doe now understands the process and is committed to "wash, rinse, and repeat" as they say in the marketplace. In other words, he becomes a faithful tither and repeats this process every opportunity he gets. If John remains faithful to God's instructions in Malachi Chapter 3, his storehouse will never lack, and he will no longer be dependent on the world's economy or bound by its systems. Tithing is one of the best biblical principles—because the Word of God is unchanging. It does not evolve to suit our preferences or adapt to our circumstances. It remains constant.

Now, let's address the question of where your tithe goes. Once you bring your tithe to church, where does that money go? Many Christians, or "Sunday Christians," like to ask that question, and it is a legitimate question, especially if you are a new, born-again Christian. We can say that the principle in the Old Testament still applies today. In the Old Testament, the tribe of priests (the Levites) were not allowed to work; their only job was to serve in the temple. God instructed Moses that tithing would be a wage for the Levites. Today, we have modern-day Levites in the form of pastors, evangelists, apostles, doctors, and prophets. They are called to full-time ministry, and their only job is to serve God in their given ministries. You give your tithe to your church, and the local church is now responsible for paying the pastors and anyone else who is in full-time ministry. It is also the church's responsibility to ensure there is bread in the house of the Lord.

A church with religious doctrine is not a suitable place to bring your tithes and offerings. Jesus did not come to Earth to create a religion, and God is not religious! Therefore, find a church that teaches Jesus Christ as the Savior and the Lord. This is important. You would not want to take your money to your local laundromat, put it in the washer, leave the laundromat, and two days later come back expecting your money to still be there as you left it, and certainly not multiplied. Why? Because your local laundromat doesn't guarantee the safety of your money. They will never guarantee that when you come back, your money will be waiting for you plus dividends.

However, if you take your money to the bank, you can leave it with them for as long as you want, knowing that at any time, you can go back and ask for it. You feel safe with the bank because they give you their word. A religious church is like a laundromat. Why would you want to sow your seed in a religious church that is disconnected from God's storehouse and expect to receive abundantly? Hold on now! You sow in a broken house (religion) where the thorns suffocate the crops. Now you want to run to that treasure house to ask for bread and expect them to give it to you? That "ain't" right (pardon my grammar). How do you distinguish between a house devoid of windows and a house designated as the dwelling place of God? Well, it's quite simple. You bring your tithes and offerings to the place where they believe and teach God is the Creator of heaven and earth; we come to Him through His Son Jesus Christ only, and the anointing of the Holy Spirit. If you happen to attend a church that does not adhere to these biblical principles, fails to teach them, or mixes God, Jesus, and the Holy Spirit with humans or other deities, then it is advisable to take your tithes and offerings and run. Run like your life depended on it because it does. I emphasize this because where you bring your tithes and offerings is a matter of great spiritual significance, impacting your life in many ways. By directing your tithes to the storehouse on Earth, you gain access to the treasure house in heaven and receive the abundance in yours. Simple as that!

The Spiritual Impact Behind the Tithes Now

I mentioned that where you bring your tithes and offerings matters and that it could have a spiritual impact on your life. So, let's talk about that spiritual impact. What happens when you pay your tithes? Every time you pay your tithes, you are putting God to the test. He told us in

Malachi 3:10: "Prove me now herewith" (KJV). Again, this is the only verse in the entire Bible where God permits you to test Him. If God says to test Him in something, the one and only Great Almighty God, I will take Him at His Word and do just that. Test Him on it! In fact, I do, and I will continue to do so. He will continue to deliver abundance in my life.

I am a living witness to the success of this principle. Yes, I have tested God with my tithes and offerings multiple times. I can tell you He is not a man that He should lie, neither the Son of man that He should repent (Numbers 23:19 KJV). He delivers every time. By God's grace, my house is not financially cursed, and it will never be cursed as long as I am putting God to this test. I am not worried about any global financial crisis that I call d.i.r.e. What is dire? Depression, inflation, recession, and emptiness. I am not worried about it at all! It does not impact me. While the world is experiencing the impact of the financial or economic crisis, I am counting my blessings in the heavenly treasure house. Each day, I wake up to find food on the table and my light bill paid. Furthermore, my wife and children are in good health and sleep peacefully every night. How is this possible? It is not due to my own power, knowledge, or a well-paying job, nor is it because I have a large bank account. No, it is because I consistently put my faith in God. Every time, I faithfully pay my tithes and offerings to the house of the Lord.

This principle truly works, my friends. Tithing is, in fact, a biblical teaching. Therefore, do not be swayed by those who claim that it is not biblical to tithe because we are under grace. They will argue that tithing is an Old Testament principle. Pause for a moment and consider this: isn't the Old Testament the inspired Word of God? Even in Malachi 3:6, which these anti-tithers disregard, it says, "I, the Lord, do not change." Additionally, in the Old Testament, God declares that His Word will never return to Him void. God's Word is eternal; it exists outside the confines of time. Being a spiritual entity, God is not bounded by time. He is eternal and operates in a timeless realm. Therefore, when God speaks or decrees a word, it remains relevant for all eternity. Although we perceive and receive His word within the constraints of time on Earth, the word itself is timeless. Thus, there is no distinction between ancient and modern words merely because we have divided the Bible into two parts: the Old and New Testaments.

I firmly believe that God allowed the Bible to have two parts to make it easier for us to understand the revelation of Jesus. Jesus was concealed before His birth in the natural realm but has since become the revealed Christ whom we presently believe in and receive. This understanding holds true for today at this very moment.

The Word of God is constant, present now and forever. As omnipresent as He is, so is His Word. Nowhere in the Bible does it say that some of God's words have an expiration date. No, it is now! The moment you open the Bible, whether it is the Old Testament or the New Testament, God is speaking to you in the present time. At that moment, you may not understand it, but He is still speaking to you now.

The revelation of God's Word can come in many forms from any of the 66 books of the Bible, whether in the Old Testament or the New Testament. The revelation of the Bible comes from our counselor and teacher, the Holy Spirit. We all need Him to teach us, open our eyes, and reveal the hidden mysteries of His Word, now! Jesus fulfilled the law, which includes the Old Testament, and the New Testament is now Christ revealed, with Him being present among us. When you dismiss the fact that tithing is a biblical principle, you make God a liar, rendering His every word obsolete. Remember that the last book of the Bible, Revelation, warns us not to add or take anything away from Scripture. By dismissing the principle of tithing, you are essentially removing a word from God's Word, both literally and figuratively.

CHAPTER 2

DISMISSING THE TITHING PRINCIPLE

Why do some Christians completely dismiss the biblical principle of tithing? This mindset is truly unbelievable. Some preachers are telling their congregations that this principle, clearly outlined in dedicated chapters and verses of the Bible they read and teach from, is not actually biblical. It is mind-boggling to hear this. They base their argument on the instructions God gave to the Levites regarding tithing. Yet, they completely disregard the principle of tithing as a whole.

The Chapter That Divides Christians

Malachi Chapter 3 has divided Christians from all walks of life. Church leaders who doubt the law of tithing are preaching to their church members that this chapter on tithing is "not biblical," even though the book of Malachi and its chapters are part of the Bible. Anti-tithers claim that paying tithes was for the Jews under the Mosaic laws in the Old Testament. Do you know what else existed in the time of Moses? Three of the four principles of giving: first fruits, alms, and charity. These are part of the Moses era and beyond, which anti-tithers are okay with. They have no problem asking for or accepting offerings or donations at the end of each mid-week and Sunday service. They reason that since we are now under grace, Malachi Chapter 3 and any other verses in the Old Testament that discuss tithing are irrelevant; therefore, you shouldn't pay tithes at church. They also teach their members that the reason pastors and God's servants ask for tithes is because they want to enrich themselves. Basically, they are accusing other ministers of scamming the children of God and making the church their "cash cow."

One of the main reasons I decided to write this book is to address this very issue and emphasize the importance of paying tithes. I believe that teaching against the biblical principle of tithing is doing a great disservice to the body of Christ. Frankly, it's because of these types of teachings that the body of Christ cannot access the treasures of God that He has stored for us in His storehouse.

I am offering my perspective, not as a pastor, prophet, doctor, or evangelist, but as a born-again Christian who believes that the Bible is the true Word of God from Genesis 1:1 to Revelation 22:21. What God instructs us to do in His book cannot be dismissed or contradicted. We must teach as it is written, regardless of whether it is in the Old Testament or the New Testament. There are no ifs or buts about it. So, when preachers explain why they don't believe in paying tithes, but then turn around and ask their congregations to bring offerings or contribute to support church activities, they are being contradictory.

The instruction to bring offerings can be found in Malachi 3:9, right next to the word "tithes." It says to bring tithes and offerings to the storehouse. If tithing is considered an Old Testament principle, then offerings should be as well. In any case, if we accept one and reject the other, then this passage in Malachi Chapter 3 becomes irrelevant. It doesn't make sense to accept one instruction from God and reject the other when they are connected.

To quote Dr. Myron Golden, "Are you picking up what I'm putting down?"

This sort of belief, where people pick and choose what suits them, is hypocritical in my opinion. Either fulfill Malachi 3:9 by bringing tithes and offerings to the storehouse or don't. It's not a complicated choice; it's a straightforward one. It's the only way. If you tell your members not to pay tithes, then you shouldn't ask them to give offerings either. It can't be one and not the other. The storehouse should accept both tithes and offerings, not just one of them. God didn't say it was an either-or choice, even in the Mosaic laws.

I mentioned earlier that paying tithes and offerings is the only way to test God. If you take it out of the Bible and dismiss it, what other way do you have to test Him? What other tools in your arsenal can you use to test Him? Which other chapter or verse in the Bible would you use to test Him? Are we supposed to ignore it because we are under grace? Well, once again, when you ignore one word as it is written in the Bible, you invalidate the entire Bible.

If the reason for not believing in tithing is because we are non-Jews by birth or Levites by tribal affiliation, then I will show you later that all born-again Christians are Jews by birth. I'd like to believe that some of those who oppose tithing could actually be faithful tithers, but there seems to be a lack of spiritual conviction on this matter. Even if they do pay their tithes, I believe it would be more out of religious obligation. If they religiously pay their tithes on Sunday morning, they could easily stop bringing them to the storehouse once they hear the message, "You don't have to pay tithes because you are under grace, not under the law."

Hearing this message with a religious mindset would strongly resonate with them, leading them to stop paying tithes altogether. Why would they? They believe they are under grace. This message has been preached numerous times before. I always wonder why a message from a human resonates more with many Christian believers, causing them to go against the true and pure Word of God, which is clearly written in the Bible. Is it possible that the arguments and interpretation of Bible verses used to persuade people to turn away from obeying God are just extremely compelling? Or does it have more to do with the condition of a person's heart? I would say the latter!

God said in Malachi 3:7, "You have turned away from my decrees and have not kept them." It's a matter of the heart, not persuasive tactics. People make this decision based on the condition of their hearts. The compelling message only reinforces and facilitates a decision that people already believe in their hearts.

So, as a Christian, which message do you believe? The unadulterated Word of God as written in the Bible, or the watered-down words of a person with deceitful intentions and a "destructive agenda"?

Remember in the garden when the Devil convinced Eve to eat from the tree of good and evil, telling her that they would become like God? Well, that's because he (Satan) used the very words of God spoken to Adam and Eve in the previous chapter, but twisted them to serve his own purposes. I once heard Dr. Myron Golden say in one of his Wednesday Bible studies, "When the Devil spoke to Eve, she quoted exactly what God had instructed regarding the tree of good and evil. The serpent added one word: 'You will **NOT** surely die,' the serpent said to the woman." It's the same trick he uses when it comes to the verse in Malachi 3:8 regarding tithing. This time, he removed tithing and left only offerings. Can you see it now? As I mentioned earlier, those who oppose tithing tell their congregations that it's not biblical, but they still insist they give offerings. Let's revisit Malachi 3:8 as it is written: "Will a mere mortal rob God? Yet you rob me. But you ask, 'How are we robbing you?' 'In tithes and offerings.'"

But, if I have to teach against tithing by using Malachi 3:8, it will look like this.

"Will a mere mortal rob God? Yet you rob me. "But you ask, 'How are we robbing you?' **"In offerings."**

You see, all you need to do to make a compelling and persuasive argument is to remove a word. The content of the message then changes its intent, affecting the condition of one's heart and one's interpretation of the new message. This is exactly what the serpent did to persuade Eve to eat from the tree of good and evil. These teachers also use this technique by manipulating the message to suit their agenda, thereby diminishing its spiritual impact. It is easier to persuade a group of followers when only one word is taken out instead of two. This demonstrates the power of subtraction or addition versus nullification. Nullification exposes false doctrine, making it easier for people to reject. However, when you subtract a word, it leaves a question mark in the hearts of followers. By removing both tithing and offering, persuasive communication becomes challenging to transmit, even for the least committed followers. I believe this is exactly what the serpent did in the garden of Eden when he quoted the Word of God to Eve, adding a slight twist to it.

So, why remove tithing and not offering? I believe it is because tithing carries more financial weight and spiritual significance. It is easier to give a $20 offering at church compared to $200 in tithes. Similarly, it is easier to give $200 in offering than $2,000 in tithing. We could even argue that giving a $20,000 offering is easier than giving $2 million in tithing. Let's use an example: if you earn $2,000 a month, your 10 percent tithes would be at least $200. However, a $20 offering is a personal decision without a specific percentage attached. So, the amount of your offering is entirely up to you. Giving $20 from a $2,000 income is an easy decision to make. It is not the same as giving everything you have, like the widow Jesus singled out in Mark 12:43. In that case, you gave one percent or even less of your overall income. It is better to give something rather than nothing, but it is not as impressive or impactful.

You are free to give any amount of offering if it is your best. The same goes for tithing. The tenth is the basis to give because that's what Abraham gave to Melchizedek. That's what Jacob promised God and that's what the law stated. I believe that under grace, you are free to give more than 10 percent. Yes, you can give 90 percent in tithing and keep ten percent for yourself, if your heart leads you in this direction in relation to God. Many Christians have vowed to give more than ten percent of their revenues or earnings in tithes to God, and they have been or are blessed beyond their imagination. I believe anyone can do so if their hearts lead them.

God rejected Cain's offering and accepted Abel's, not because He is a meat lover and hates vegetables but due to the condition of Cain's heart. Both brothers presented offerings to God, likely what they considered their best. However, they approached their altars with different conditions of the heart.

The Devil knows he can't completely convince the multitude who love God and believe in Jesus Christ as Savior and Lord not to bring their tithes and offerings to the storehouse. Instead, he targets those who will replenish the storehouse the most. The Devil is a liar. He used the same trick in both the first book of the Old Testament (Genesis) and the last book (Malachi). Unfortunately, some Christians are still persuaded by the preaching of other preachers. Here's an example: the Devil attempted to use this trick in the first book of the New Testament (Matthew). Do you remember when the Spirit of God took Jesus to the desert to fast for 40 days and 40 nights? Guess who came to tempt Jesus using the same trick he used on Eve and in Malachi Chapter 3? The Devil in the flesh. He tried this with Jesus after He completed His 40 days of fasting.

The Devil knows the Scriptures well and presents his message while adding his own twist to it. You see, when you give a new message to someone who is going through challenging times, staying within the current message, it is difficult to receive pushback or be questioned, especially if the listener has little knowledge of the Bible compared to the speaker. They call it "new revelation" to soften the blow when it lands in one's incredulous heart. That is what the Devil understood, and that is why he was able to be so persuasive. Adam and Eve were willing to go against God's will because, in their minds, the serpent was right. They believed it was still godly to eat the fruit, even though they were already like God. They were eternal spirits, fruitful, multipliers, subduers, and dominants, and most importantly, they were made in the image of God. (Genesis 1:26: "Let us make man in our image.") But Eve did not discern it and took a bite of the fruit. One destructive message led to self-destruction, and it had a domino effect on mankind through time until Jesus came to restore what the Devil stole in the garden of Eden. Alleluia! Praise God!

I believe the Devil attacks Malachi 3:9 because he doesn't want believers to test God. He knows that if they do so, they will be blessed beyond their imaginations, just as God promises. This would harm the world system that he has set up. He knows that God doesn't lie, so he doesn't want believers to be blessed by their heavenly Father. Instead, he wants to make them believe that his system in this world is the only way to be self-sufficient and succeed. He wants believers to doubt and question the Word of God, just as he did with Eve in the garden of Eden. He doesn't want them to believe in him directly because that would be unacceptable to many Christians. Instead, he wants them to believe in the system that Kenneth Copeland called "The Babylonian System." He is the destroyer and the master of confusion. Can we expect anything less from him?

What is the twist?

CHAPTER 3

ANTI-TITHERS AND SKEPTICAL CHRISTIANS

I have debated the subject of tithing many times before with relatives and people close to me who don't believe in the principle of tithing but to no avail. They remain firm in their beliefs, as the message they've received aligns with their convictions. So, what could possibly be said to change their minds? There is nothing that can be done to sway them. We can only pray and believe that God alone will undo what needs to be undone in their hearts for them to understand there is no such thing as the "old Word of God and new Word of God." God's Word is now. It is the same yesterday, today, and tomorrow.

I have started studying this subject in depth with the help of the Holy Spirit because tithing has become a recurring subject that I debate, and I will likely continue to debate with many Christians. I have delved into a thorough examination of tithing in the Bible and have tried to understand the arguments from the other side. I have sought an objective approach to this subject and wanted to know why some are so dismissive of this issue. I hope that by learning and understanding this subject clearly with the help of the

Holy Spirit, God will use me to touch people's hearts and bring them back to Him, as He said in Malachi Chapter 3. It is a big deal for me to spend time on this issue because I know the impact of tithes in the spiritual and natural realms. I strongly believe in tithing, and I am a living testimony of its blessings in my life and my wife's life. But before I dive into sharing my testimony, I want to stay on the topic of anti-tithers and skeptical Christians regarding tithing.

Throughout my time sharing and debating the message of tithing with other Christians and listening to others speak about it, I have come to realize that their arguments are similar regardless of their religious affiliation or geographical location. They all have the same four main arguments against tithing:

- It's a form of a scam that preachers use to steal money from their members.
- Fake and prosperity preachers use these Old Testament verses to enrich themselves to build their mega-churches.
- It's part of prosperity preaching for modern-day preachers.
- Christianity is a poor people's religion and these preachers prey on them and steal their money by promising them wealth if they pay their tithes and offerings.

These are the arguments typically given to justify not paying tithes to the local church and to express their stance on this topic. However, as previously mentioned, tithing is intricately connected to one's heart. Again, God accepted

Abel's offering and rejected Cain's not because of the quantity, but because of the condition of their hearts. One brother's heart was aligned with God, while the other brother's heart harbored animosity toward his sibling. The conditions of the heart include jealousy, hate, envy, and selfishness, among others. Conversely, the opposite conditions are justice, mercy, and faithfulness.

In Matthew Chapter 23, Jesus criticized the teachers of the law and the Pharisees regarding both tithing and the condition of their hearts. Although they faithfully paid their tithes, they neglected the most essential aspect of giving: the heart. Jesus did not condemn them for tithing because they were fulfilling the law, which is commendable. Rather, he reminded them that while giving is important, it is equally important to give with a joyful heart. The intention of the offering and the condition of the heart must align before the act of offering itself, so that God may find the offering favorable. Jesus never dismisses the act of tithing. In fact, the only time he directly discussed tithing was to remind us how to tithe: by practicing justice, mercy, and faithfulness without neglecting it.

"Woe to you, teachers of the law and Pharisees, you hypocrites! You give a tenth of your spices—mint, dill, and cumin. But you have neglected the more important matters of the law—justice, mercy, and faithfulness. You should have practiced the latter without neglecting the former. You blind guides! You strain out a gnat but swallow a camel" (Matthew 23:23-24 NIV).

Neglecting the heart, as Jesus reminded us, has been an ongoing issue since the recording of the first offering. There is no doubt that God loved both Abel and Cain. He spoke to one brother, warning him to release any resentment in his heart toward his sibling. Unfortunately, he was unable to do so, resulting in the hardening of his heart. Nevertheless, God never rejected Cain personally; He simply rejected his offering, just as he may reject our tithing. God will not reject us for failing to give our tithes, but He will reject our tithes if we neglect to let go of what is in our hearts. Before giving our tithes, we must have hearts characterized by justice, mercy, and faithfulness. Cain neglected this crucial aspect, and quite frankly, his heart was consumed by rage. Hence, he killed his brother Abel. Do you know that Cain killed his brother Abel after Abel had given his offering to God? This was the first murder ever committed by mankind. The first human was killed over an offering. Now you understand why the Devil wants you to stay in poverty, struggles and lack. If he can entice a man to kill another man over an offering, that means it's a very significant matter, folks. You do not want to disregard this tithing principle.

God loves believers whose hearts are fully devoted to Him. Second Corinthians 7:9 says that God loves a cheerful giver. God loves it when you make an offering with a cheerful heart. That's what Abel did, and Cain did not. David was many things to God and performed many acts, including giving offerings. Therefore, God called David "a man after my own heart," and He called Jesus "my beloved son in whom I am well pleased."

Dr. Myron Golden is an entrepreneur, pastor, and mentor who has helped many entrepreneurs in the marketplace achieve six to seven-figure income in less time by applying the biblical principles that King Solomon applied in his day. He said that David's name means "beloved one," and when Jesus was baptized, a voice came down from heaven and said, "This is my beloved son." When he shared this revelation, I received it. So, God called David "the beloved one" and "a man after my own heart", and when Jesus was baptized, a voice came down from heaven and said, "This is my beloved son in whom I am well pleased." If we replace the word "beloved" with the name "David" in this verse, this is what God is saying: "You had your David, but this one is the real David in whom I am well pleased."

David and Jesus had three main things in common:

1. They were both kings, with Jesus still being the King
2. They had hearts fully committed to God and would only move when God said, "GO!"
3. They never lost a battle. Alleluia!

How could men like these have their offerings rejected by God? It's impossible. They are connected to God and the resources of God's kingdom because they have a God's heart. Ask God to give you a heart of flesh. Fix your heart before giving any offering, and you, too, can be like David and Jesus. You will be connected to God, and you will never lose a battle. Alleluia!

So, having a heart fully devoted to God and His things is what unlocks the windows of heaven to receive your tithes and offerings. We can all be like little David by following the example of the second David and believing that the Bible is His Word, which remains the same yesterday, today, and forever. If I had to connect this sentence with random chapters from the Bible, it would sound like this: "The book of Genesis Chapter 1 is the same as yesterday, today, and tomorrow; Psalm 1 is the same yesterday, today, and tomorrow; 2 Corinthians Chapter 9 is the same yesterday, today, and tomorrow, and Malachi Chapter 3 is the same yesterday, today, and tomorrow. I reiterate that there is no such thing as "old God's Word" and "new God's Word" even though we have a Bible that is divided in two parts, an Old Testament and New Testament. All of God's words are forever now!

Three Types of Non-Tithers

We have identified the four main reasons why Christians who do not believe in tithing do not give their tithes. I have come up with three types of characteristics of non-tithers. These characteristics enable them to justify not giving their tithes to the Lord.

The Non-Tither

Three kinds of Christians are non-tithers:

1. **The incredulous Christians:** no matter what you tell them, they still won't be persuaded that tithing is a biblical thing to do, even though it is clearly written in the Bible. They don't believe in it, and they think it's a scam preachers use to enrich themselves.

2. **The Stingy Christians:** they think that taking 10 percent of their income and bringing it to church is outrageous. They don't want to make the pastor rich, and they believe that their household budget will be impacted if they bring their tithes to church. They have prioritized expenses and taking money out of this budget to pay their tithes will make a dent and even leave a hole in

their finances. They believe they have better things to do with that money.

3. **The Ignorant Christians:** since they were born again, they have never been taught the principle of tithing or simply don't understand it. In a sense, it's not their fault. The church has failed this category of people. I am certain that once correctly taught, this category of Christians will have no problem bringing their tithes to the storehouse.

Two Types of Tithers

Once Christians understand the spiritual impact of tithing (because they have been taught or they have studied deeply on their own and have no doubt this is the Word of God that we must honor for our own good) they will have no issues. However, when there is an issue that impacts their giving, despite their belief in it, that's when we have to sort out these believers based on their level of faith regarding this subject.

The Sparing Tither

Sparing tithers are those who believe in tithing but prioritize everything else. They show restraint with their money due to various reasons. When they earn an income, they prioritize other needs such as bills, food, and entertainment over tithes and offerings. Only when they have a surplus in their revenue and have taken care of all their other obligations do they give their tithes. Their giving is based on what they will have left after taking care of everything else. Like stingy Christians, sparing tithers believe in tithing but allow circumstances to affect their giving. However, unlike stingy Christians who have more than enough but still choose not to tithe, sparing tithers believe that we shouldn't give tithes because we live under grace and not under the law.

The Faithful Tither

The faithful tither is a "total package" Christian who understands the principle of tithing. This is the type of Christian we should all aspire to be. Regardless of their circumstances, their first priority is to give God a tithe and offering and not worry about the rest. They understand that money can't solve their problems. Tithes take precedence, no matter what. They know that God understands what they are going through and what is in their bank accounts. However, they give anyway because they know that by giving, they are honoring the Word of God and putting Him to the test as He commands when it comes to bringing tithes to the storehouse. The faithful tithers get excited and rejoice when it's time to give their tithes. They also know the Devil hates it because he can't touch them once their finances are in God's hands. They believe that even under grace, we should pay our tithes with cheerful hearts. This is not the common, legalistic form of tithing seen in the Mosaic law but a spiritual act of worship to God.

CHAPTER 4

MY TESTIMONY

I was once a non-tither, and I lived with the financial consequences of this decision. I consider it a decision because it was. At that time, it felt like every step forward I took resulted in two to three steps backward. I was always broke. When I received my biweekly pay check, I would have money in my wallet or bank account, but by the end of the week, it was all gone. I didn't even know where the money went. I was living proof of what happens when you rob God in plain sight as written in Malachi Chapter 3. One minute I had money, the next minute it was gone. I was a sparing tither because I only pretended to tithe when I had some money left after paying all my bills. If I was tight on money for that week, tithing would have to wait. But when was that next time? That was up to me, and only if I had enough. That's robbing God. And yes, I robbed Him, and I paid the price financially, physically, and spiritually. Proverbs 23:5 has something to say about people like me: "In the blink of an eye, wealth disappears, for it will sprout wings and fly away like an eagle."

The only time I faithfully tithed was during my deployment in Iraq in 2007. When I set foot on Iraqi soil, I didn't feel nervous or afraid of entering a combat zone and not knowing if I would come back in a body bag. In fact, stepping foot in Iraq filled me with awe and inspiration. This land was full of history. Our father Abraham and other champions of faith walked on this land. However, I also realized that despite its rich history, it was now a war zone, and there was a possibility that I might not make it out alive. The possibility of returning in a body bag existed.

The Covenant

Many brave individuals had fallen during this war. Most of these fallen heroes were much better than me. I was realistic about this and accepted the reality. So, I made a covenant with God. Before deploying, our command's chaplain distributed small New Testament Bibles with desert camouflage covers (See figure 3 Below) to the crew in my squadron. When I arrived in Iraq, I placed this small Bible in the left pocket of my desert camouflage uniform. After realizing that I could potentially leave this historic land, now a war zone, in a body bag, I decided to make a covenant with God. This was my covenant to Him: "Lord, I don't know if I will make it out of here dead or alive. Only You know. But if I came here to die, this is how I want to go. I will carry this small Bible in my left pocket every day while I am here. If I came here to die, I want the bullet that kills me to pierce my heart after it pierces through this Bible that I am holding, Your Word. But if You keep me alive until the end, I will pay tithes on every earning I receive while I am on this land."

Figure 3: My military issued New Testament Bible

That was the covenant I made with God during my first and second deployments in Iraq. God honored the covenant. He kept me alive. I am not better than the fallen heroes, but He protected me, and I am honored. I did not neglect my duty to God during my deployments. I paid my tithes. Like the late Kenneth Hagin used to say, "I did, and He did."

That was the only time I was faithful in paying my tithes then. After my deployments, I returned to my old ways of paying sparingly or not paying at all, and I fell back into the same hole of lack as before. Meaning that one minute I had money and the next minute I was broke. Fast forward to when my wife and I got married in 2010, I was still stuck in my old ways. This time, I had the responsibility of taking care of my better half and preparing for the birth of our first child, my son Davin. I started prioritizing my finances and there was no room for tithing in my budget. This continued throughout 2010.

One day in the freezing winter of December, as I came back from work late in the evening and settled down after a long day, my wife came to sit next to me. She told me that while she was praying during the day, God had told her to tell me that I needed to start paying my tithes. My wife is a spiritual woman and more of a prayer warrior than I am, so it made perfect sense for God to speak to her. As the sole breadwinner of the household at that time, the responsibility to start paying our tithes fell on me. Thank God for our Spirit-filled Christian wives. Once I heard this from my wife, I decided to become the faithful tither I should have been a long time ago, the person God expected me to be since I have always believed in this principle. No more prioritizing everything else before paying our tithes, no matter what.

You read my testimony. But have you ever wondered why non-believers always seem to prosper? They don't pray; they don't believe in a living God, they don't even believe in tithing, and they don't honor God. Some are even wicked, Devil worshippers, and greedy. Yet, for some reason, they always seem to prosper in everything they do. Meanwhile, Christians who believe in the Word of God from Genesis Chapter 1 to Revelation Chapter 22 live in poverty and lack spiritual impact. How is this possible?

Well, there is a reason for it. God is very strict with us Christians because He loves us. We have a relationship of a father and a son. He allows judgment to come upon us in our lives while we are still on Earth so that we can remember the love of the Father and return to His will, just as the Prodigal Son did. He allows the wicked to prosper and live large because they have no relationship with Him as a Father, and their judgment awaits them at the end of the day. Malachi Chapter 3 wasn't written for the wicked. It does not apply to them. It was written for you and me, the believers. That's why we cannot and should not envy the wicked. God warned us not to be like them.

Now listen, you rich people, weep and wail because of the misery that is coming on you. ² Your wealth has rotted, and moths have eaten your clothes. ³ Your gold and silver are corroded. Their corrosion will testify against you and eat your flesh like fire. You have hoarded wealth in the last days. ⁴ Look! The wages you failed to pay the workers who mowed your fields are crying out against you. The cries of the harvesters have reached the ears of the Lord Almighty. ⁵ You have lived on earth in luxury and self-indulgence. You have fattened yourselves in the day of slaughter. [a] ⁶ You have condemned and murdered the innocent one, who was not opposing you. (James 5:1-6)

The pests devouring crops as it is written in Malachi 3:12 is the result of stealing from God by not bringing tithes and offerings to His storehouse. This should be an eye-opener for every Christian who has a relationship with God. The lack in your life is a wake-up call that you need to return to your Father, where even His servants do not lack. This is not just an Old Testament matter or a message addressed only to the Levites as some preachers suggest. This is the Word spoken by a deity who dwells outside of time, a deity whom the universe cannot contain. Therefore, every word from Genesis Chapter 1 to the end of Revelation Chapter 22 is relevant in the present.

CHAPTER 5

THE ORIGIN OF TITHING

For the sake of analogy, we like to say that the Old Testament is the New Testament concealed, and the New Testament is the Old Testament revealed. We also say that the Old Testament is the shadow of Jesus Christ, and the New Testament is the body of Christ. This means that there is no separation between the two. There is not even a millimeter of daylight between these two books. It's all one

If the Old Testament is the shadow of Christ, then let us dig deep into the Old Testament regarding the origin of tithing and find out what caused it to be an issue that divides Christians now.

After Abram returned from defeating Kedorlaomer and the kings allied with him, the king of Sodom came out to meet him in the Valley of Shaveh (that is, the King's Valley). Then Melchizedek king of Salem brought out bread and wine. He was the priest of God Most High, and he blessed Abram, saying, "Blessed be Abram by God Most High, Creator of heaven and earth. And praise be to God Most High, who delivered your enemies into your hand."Then Abram gave him a tenth of everything. (Genesis 14:17-20)

Let's address the question of Abraham giving a tenth of

everything to Melchizedek. Where did Abraham learn about the practice of tithing? Abraham came from the land of Ur, a place where the Chaldeans worshiped other gods. It is possible that his father was an idol worshiper. In any religion, believers tend to offer their best to their gods, a practice that has been followed throughout history. They paid taxes and brought offerings to their gods, sometimes even giving a tenth of their produce or more. Being a native of Ur, Abraham probably learned about the principle of tithing from his father's land.

My brothers and sisters, this was the environment in which Abraham lived for 75 years of his life. Seventy-five years is a long time to develop habits. His title as the "Father of Faith" stems from his willingness to heed the command and listen to the voice of the true, living God amidst the sea of gods, ultimately leading him to depart from his father's land and venture into the realm of the unknown. It takes faith to make a decision like this.

Sorry, I digress. Let's return to our main subject. The first time a form of offering described as a tenth is mentioned in the Bible is in Genesis 14:20. We can agree that it was the first time a man gave a tenth of everything to God, the Creator of heaven and earth, and not to the other gods of that time.

The Hebrew word for tithe is *ma'aser*, which means the tenth of the produce. Why is it mentioned for the first time in Genesis Chapter 14? Well, let's take a step back. When Abraham saw Melchizedek, the King of Salem and a priest of the God Most High, come to him and bless him, he knew that he was in the presence of a deity. But this deity was different from the other deities in his hometown. This deity was the "big G," the Creator of heaven and earth. This deity had no mother or father and could not be seen by man and live, unlike the other gods that were created in the image of their worshipers. I am not assuming that Abraham knew who Melchizedek was; I know this because he declared it in Genesis 14:21-22.

"The king of Sodom said to Abram, 'Give me the people and keep the goods for yourself.' But Abram said to the king of Sodom, 'With raised hand I have sworn an oath to the Lord, God Most High, Creator of heaven and earth'" (Genesis 14:19).

When Melchizedek blessed Abram in verse 19, he received the revelation that he was standing in the presence of a supreme being. The Bible identifies this being as the King of Salem (King of Peace) and a priest of God Most High. He predated all mankind, and Abram's old religious instinct was to give an offering. This time, it was out of the question to give the tenth to the gods, but to give the tenth of everything to The God.

Have you ever noticed that it is easier for a Muslim who is a born-again Christian to pray three times a day or fast for 30 days than for a Christian who was raised in the church? Well, that's just a religious instinct they continue to practice when they become Christians. They even become more spiritual Christians than born-again Christians who were born and raised in Christian homes. That is the reason why Abraham, who had never attended a Bible school or a church and had never offered anything significant to God like Noah and Abel, reinstated the practice of ma'aser on that very day by giving a tenth of everything to Melchizedek. As the Father of Faith, Abraham restored ma'aser to its rightful place so that all his descendants could follow his example and bring a tenth of everything to the Lord, God Most High, the Creator of heaven and earth.

God never mentioned to Abraham that the great nations would come from him before he gave a tenth of everything to Melchizedek. Genesis 15:1 begins with "After this." He found out that the nations would come from his offspring in Genesis 15:1-7 and made a covenant with God in Genesis 15:18-21 "After this." Let's read:

After this, the word of the LORD came to Abram in a vision: "Do not be afraid, Abram. I am your shield, your very great reward."

2 But Abram said, "Sovereign LORD, what can you give me since I remain childless and the one who will inherit my estate is Eliezer of Damascus?" 3 And Abram said, "You have given me no children; so a servant in my household will be my heir."

4 Then the word of the LORD came to him: "This man will not be your heir, but a son who is your own flesh and blood will be your heir." 5 He took him outside and said, "Look up at the sky and count the stars—if indeed you can count them." Then he said to him, "So shall your offspring be."

6 Abram believed the LORD, and he credited it to him as righteousness.

7 He also said to him, "I am the LORD, who brought you out of Ur of the Chaldeans to give you this land to take possession of it."

God was pleased with Abraham's offering, so He appeared to him in a vision. They discussed the issue of offspring. However, in Genesis 14:20, when Abraham gave a tenth of everything, he did not tell Melchizedek, "This tenth of all that I offer to you is for me and all my descendants for generations to come." No! It was a worship offering, the best from his heart. In the process, Abraham reinstated tithing to its rightful place so that we can do the same.

One of the arguments I have heard from Christians who do not believe in tithing is that we do not need to pay our tithes because Father Abraham gave a tenth of everything to Melchizedek on behalf of all us Christians, who are spiritual heirs of Father Abraham.

I could not disagree more with this argument! You see, Abraham is the father of faith, not the savior of the faithful. Jesus Christ is the Savior. He is all that and the only One who paid a one-time price for all of us—the ultimate price. No other person has paid or will ever pay a one-time price of any kind for mankind, except Jesus. Abraham set an example for all of us to follow: we should love God with everything we have. Yes, even the Isaac in your life. Be prepared to offer everything to God. No ifs, ands, or buts about it. You should come to God with everything, and you should worship Him with everything.

Let's revisit Genesis 15:5 together: "He took him outside and said, 'Look up at the sky and count the stars—if indeed you can count them.' Then he said to him, 'So shall your offspring be.'"

At that moment, Abram found out about the nations that would come from him. But right after that, Sarai gave Hagar to Abram so she could bear him an heir. Well, Ishmael was indeed Abram's descendant, so he had the right to the lands that God named in verses 18-21.

"On that day the <u>Lord</u> made a covenant with Abram and said, 'To your descendants I give this land, from the Wadi of Egypt to the great river, the Euphrates— [19] the land of the Kenites, Kenizzites, Kadmonites, [20] Hittites, Perizzites, Rephaites, [21] Amorites, Canaanites, Girgashites and Jebusites'" (Genesis 15:18-21).

Ishmael came into possession of this covenant, and to this day, his descendants dwell in the land of Egypt. Later, Abraham had six more children who were also part of this covenant, and they too dwelled in the lands stated in verse 18.

God did not speak to Abram for 13 years because he decided to take matters of offspring into his own hands and had Ishmael. Thirteen years later, at the age of 99, God finally spoke to Abram, and everything changed. God declared a new covenant with Abram. This time, He only named Canaan and revealed that in this new covenant, not only would He make Abram great nations, but kings would come from him. God did not decree that kings would come from Abram before Ishmael. He decreed this, 13 years after the first covenant, the pre-Ishmael covenant. However, the covenant post-Ishmael to Abraham is the covenant that births kings. It is the covenant He reiterated to Isaac and Jacob.

As for me, this is my covenant with you: You will be the father of many nations. [5] No longer will you be called Abram[b]; your name will be Abraham,[c] for I have made you a father of many nations. [6] I will make you very fruitful; I will make nations of you, and kings will come from you. [7] I will establish my covenant as an everlasting covenant between me and you and your descendants after you for the generations to come, to be your

God and the God of your descendants after you. [8] The whole land of Canaan, where you now reside as a foreigner, I will give as an everlasting possession to you and your descendants after you; and I will be their God. (Genesis 17:4-8).

What about the six other children Abraham had with Keturah: Zimran, Jokshan, Medan, Midian, Ishbak and Shuah? It is a relevant question since I mentioned the covenant post-Ishmael. The Bible said that Abraham sent them away from his son Isaac to the land of the East.

"Abraham left everything he owned to Isaac. [6] But while he was still living, he gave gifts to the sons of his concubines and sent them away from his son Isaac to the land of the east" (Genesis 25:5).

In this covenant, He gave Abram and Sarai new names, and the covenant was attached to a new law. He revealed the name of the child Abraham would have and specifically said he would establish a covenant with Isaac. Notice Abraham never said anything about all these blessings proclaimed by God in the covenant.

After the death of Abraham, God appeared to Isaac in the time of famine in the land.

"Stay in this land for a while, and I will be with you and will bless you. For to you and your descendants I will give all these lands and will confirm the oath I swore to your father Abraham. I will make your descendants as numerous as the stars in the sky and will give them all these lands, and through your offspring, all nations on earth will be blessed" (Genesis 26:3-4).

Notice here again, Isaac never said a word regarding all

these blessings proclaimed in the covenant by God just like Abraham.

Here Comes Jacob

Jacob found himself running away from his brother after deceiving his father and stealing the blessing intended for his brother. The sun was going down, so he stopped at a place to sleep, before continuing his journey the next day. Then he had a dream.

I am the Lord, the God of your father Abraham and the God of Isaac. I will give you and your descendants the land on which you are lying. 14 Your descendants will be like the dust of the earth, and you will spread out to the west and to the east, to the north and the south. All peoples on earth will be blessed through you and your offspring.[d] 15 I am with you and will watch over you wherever you go, and I will bring you back to this land. I will not leave you until I have done what I have promised you.
(Genesis 28:3-4)

Jacob woke up and in realization said,

"Surely the LORD is in this place, and I was not aware of it." He was afraid and said, "How awesome is this place! This is none other than the house of God; this is the gate of heaven"
(Genesis 28:16-17).

He called that place Bethel early in the morning. Then he felt compelled to speak, and this act, his speech, altered the covenant of God. It became a two-way covenant, instead of just one way like it was with Adam, Noah, Abraham, and Isaac. Let's read:

If God will be with me and will watch over me on this journey I am taking and will give me food to eat and clothes to wear so that I return safely to my father's household, then the LORD will be my God and this stone that I have set up as a pillar will be God's house, and of all that you give me, I will give you a tenth (Genesis 28:20-22).

For the first time since God established covenants with men—going back to Adam (the Adamic covenant), a man altered the course of history. This new covenant led to the introduction of legalistic tithing in the Mosaic law. How did this happen? It was because of Jacob's promise. When Jacob was promised, "I will give you and your descendants the land. All the people on earth will be blessed. I have promised you," he felt compelled to make an offering right then and there. Unfortunately, he had nothing of value to offer God. So, he made a vow to give God a tenth of all that he would receive. It's worth noting that Jacob was on the run from his brother Esau and had practically nothing with him. In fact, he didn't even have a pillow to lay his head on when he stopped for the night. He used a stone as a pillow and went to sleep.

We know that God blessed Jacob when he worked for his uncle Laban, and twenty years later, he left with great wealth. Therefore, it's safe to assume that he did not fulfil his vow to give a tenth of everything God had given him as he had promised. Nowhere is it written that Jacob gave a tenth of all as he had vowed. Even if he had given a tenth of what he left with from his uncle's land, to whom did he give the tithe? In order for him to give the tenth, the high priest, Melchizedek, would have had to appear to him as he did with Abraham. However, there is no record of this encounter taking place between Jacob and Melchizedek. The only encounter Jacob had with God was a wrestling match that lasted until dawn. He didn't even take the time to give the tithe he had accumulated over the last twenty years of working for his uncle.

It's fair to say that Jacob never fulfilled the vow he made, let alone gave a tenth of the land as promised. It's important to note that out of Abraham, Isaac, and Jacob, only Jacob vowed to give a tenth of all the land. As Pastor Patrick Mubobo once said, "In the covenant, we come to give without seeking what we can receive in return." Prior to making a covenant with Jacob, God had already made covenants with four other individuals: Adam, Noah, Abraham, and Isaac. Adam, Noah, Abraham, and Isaac remained silent. God came to give, and He never asked for anything in return from them, since the covenant was one-way first. He was giving without expecting (unconditional).

The first four never bothered to even promise God something in return and make it a mutual covenant. When the covenant was decreed to Abraham and Isaac, God confirmed he would give 100 percent, expecting nothing of material value in return. But when it came to Jacob, God expected to receive because Jacob also decreed, he would give a tenth of all. Now, who taught Jacob about giving God the tenth of all? His grandfather Abraham. According to my calculations, Jacob was around 15 years old when Abraham died. So, he had a lot of conversations about giving with his grandkids (Jacob and Esau). Jacob's vow was now tied to the covenant that God made. I too made a vow once with the Lord, and I tied it to my tithe (see my testimony). You could also do what Jacob did. Make a covenant with God that you will keep no matter what and connect it to your tithing. That way, not only will you be able to honor your covenant with God, but at the same time put Him to the test, as He said, and see if He will not protect your finances, crops, and well-being.

Jacob was the first to test God. So, when he made a vow to the Lord, he activated a twofold principle. One that became a legalistic law for the people of Israel and the other a spiritual law for born-again Christians. The moment Jacob made that vow, which neither Abraham nor Isaac made, to pay a tenth of all the land God would give him, he automatically edited the original covenant, which is a decree made by the King of kings and Lord of lords. Now, the kings (all of Israel) entered an agreement through the vow (decree) made by one king (Israel). The origin of the covenant was a sole decree to be fulfilled by God at the given time. "So shall my word be that goes forth out of my mouth: it shall not return unto me void, but it shall accomplish that which I please, and it shall prosper in the thing whereto I sent it" (Isaiah 55:11 KJV).

Jacob's vow (decree) made it a two-way agreement, and that's how tithing became part of the law. The children of Israel received lands and blessings promised by Jacob (Israel). Since they are the children of Israel, they had to honor the promise their father made to God. What better way to make it a law? This way, they didn't have to be religious about it. If God had made it a religious practice, then they would have turned around and given their tithes to other gods instead of God, the Creator of heaven and earth.

Tithing is a law of government and worship. It is not a

religious practice. It never has been and never will be. If tithing were religious, under which religion did Abraham give his tithes to Melchizedek? Tithing was legalistic under the Mosaic laws, but not anymore. Now, I would say it symbolizes the honor and trust we have in God. It is about acknowledging that we are citizens of God's kingdom. It is an act of worshiping God. Yes, when coming to the house of the Lord, one should not come empty-handed. In earthly kingdoms, when summoned by a king or queen, one does not show up without a gift. This tradition of bringing an offering has been practiced in many cultures for ages. Even in the modern-day democratic system, presidents visit their counterparts and bring gifts. In the context of the United States, any gift received by the president from his counterpart(s) becomes the property of the United States. When the president's term is up, he must leave that gift behind. In the kingdom, every gift belongs to the king.

Let me give you another perspective on tithing. If you were wondering whether giving tithes is biblical or not, I would advise you to worship God with everything you have. If you apply this principle of using tithing as a form of worship, you will find yourself aligned with the Bible. You can't go wrong. Just try it. Here is a simple prayer you can use:

Heavenly Father, I bring my tithes to You as an act of worship, for You have always provided for me, and I never lack. You are the Creator of heaven and earth and all the riches therein. Silver and gold belong to You. You are the God of abundance who never lacks. Everything I own is Yours. One hundred percent of my earnings are Yours. You have the power to take it all away from me at any time, but You have allowed me to keep 90 percent. I won't just bring my tithe to You, my Lord. No, I will worship You with a tenth of everything and thank You for the 90 percent You allow me to keep. It is more than enough. I worship You with my whole being, Lord. In Jesus Christ's name. Amen!

"Verily I say unto you, Whatsoever ye shall bind on earth shall be bound in heaven: and whatsoever ye shall loose on earth shall be loosed in heaven" (Matthew 18:18).

CHAPTER 6

THE TRIBE OF LEVITES

The Lord chose Aaron and the sons of the tribe of Levi to be priests of Israel because their sole duties as priests were to take care of the tabernacle that Moses had built for God. These were their sacred duties. The duty of the Levites was to fulfil their responsibilities for the care and maintenance of the tabernacle; no one else was authorized to assist Aaron except the Levites. They were not allowed inside the sanctuary or the altar because it was the Holy of Holiest place. Only priests were allowed to enter.

Then the LORD said to Aaron: "You and your sons and your father's house with you shall bear the [a]iniquity related to the sanctuary, and you and your sons with you shall bear the iniquity associated with your priesthood. 2 Also bring with you your brethren of the tribe of Levi, the tribe of your father, that they may be joined with you and serve you while you and your sons are with you before the tabernacle of [b]witness. 3 They shall attend to your [c]needs and all the needs of the tabernacle; but they shall not come near the articles of the sanctuary and the altar, lest they die—they and you also. 4 They shall be joined with you and attend to the needs of the tabernacle of meeting, for all the work of the tabernacle; but an outsider shall not come near you. 5 And you shall attend to the duties of the sanctuary and the duties of the altar, that there may be no more wrath on the children of Israel. 6 Behold, I Myself have taken your brethren the

*Levites from among the children of Israel; they are a gift to you, given by the L*ORD*, to do the work of the tabernacle of meeting. [7] Therefore you and your sons with you shall attend to your priesthood for everything at the altar and behind the veil; and you shall serve. I give your priesthood to you as a gift for service, but the outsider who comes near shall be put to death.*
(Numbers 18:1-7)

*A tithe of everything from the land, whether grain from the soil or fruit from the trees, belongs to the L*ORD*; it is holy to the L*ORD*. Whoever would redeem any of their tithes must add a fifth of the value to it. Every tithe of the herd and flock—every tenth animal that passes under the shepherd's rod—will be holy to the L*ORD*. No one may pick out the good from the bad or make any substitution. If anyone does make a substitution, both the animal and its substitute become holy and cannot be redeemed.*
(Leviticus 27:30-33)

*When you have finished laying aside all the tithe of your increase in the third year—the year of tithing—and have given it to the Levite, the stranger, the fatherless, and the widow, so that they may eat within your gates and be filled, then you shall say before the L*ORD *your God: 'I have removed the [d]holy tithe from my house, and also have given them to the Levite, the stranger, the fatherless, and the widow, according to all Your commandments which You have commanded me; I have not transgressed Your commandments, nor have I forgotten them.*
(Deuteronomy 26:12-13).

We understand why God instructed the Israelites to give their tithes to the Levites, and the Levites were to give a tenth of the tithes to the priests. We read in the Bible about

God's instructions regarding tithing, which were for the Levites to receive the tithes and for the priests to receive a tenth of that. This law was implemented by God so that the Levites and priests could focus on their duties in the tabernacle. Tithes served as compensation for their devotion to their priestly responsibilities. Giving tithes to the Levites and priests is a way of giving to God. However, the notion that tithing is only under the law and no longer applicable since we are now under grace is preposterous. As mentioned before, giving the best of our produce has nothing to do with the law; it is a form of worshiping the Lord our God, who is the Creator of heaven and earth.

When Abraham first tithed, the law did not exist yet. He tithed to a priest named Melchizedek. The law instructed Israel to tithe to the priests. Jesus, during his time on Earth, lived under the law, and He came to fulfil it, not to abolish it. Therefore, Jesus paid His tithes to the Levites, just as He paid His taxes to the Roman empire.

"Give back to Caesar what is Caesar's and to God what is God's"
(Mark 12:17).

The Ten Commandments were given to the Jews, not to born-again Christians. However, Jesus fulfilled those commandments on our behalf and gave His life so that we could have eternal life. The law does not make one "holy"; in fact, it brings death. Once you break one law, you have broken them all. As born-again Christians, we are no longer under the condemnation of the law given by Moses; we are now under grace and have the nature of Christ. He is the embodiment of the law, and His law is written in our hearts.

"This is the covenant I will make with the people of Israel after that time," declares the Lord. "I will put my law in their minds and write it on their hearts. I will be their God, and they will be my people" (Jeremiah 31:33).

Just as the law of tithing was established for the Levites and priests, in the New Testament, Jesus is portrayed as the high priest to whom Abraham presented tithes and received a blessing in return. He is referred to as the King of Salem, a place associated with peace, and His origins remain unknown. He is described as having neither a beginning nor an end.

This Melchizedek was king of Salem and priest of God Most High. He met Abraham returning from the defeat of the kings and blessed him, [2] and Abraham gave him a tenth of everything. First, the name Melchizedek means "king of righteousness"; then also, "king of Salem" means "king of peace." [3] Without father or mother, without genealogy, without beginning of days or end of life, resembling the Son of God, he remains a priest forever.
(Hebrews 7:1-3 NIV)

If Abraham, who was not bound by the law, gave his tithes to the one without origin, the King of Salem (Jesus the concealed High Priest), why would you not want to give your tithes to Jesus Christ (the revealed High Priest)? During Abraham's time, there were no Levite priests because they were within Abraham. There were no tabernacles to maintain or altars to offer sacrifices to redeem the sins of the people and the priests themselves, as there was no law and therefore no sins to cleanse legally. Abraham obediently followed God and walked by faith. He was the friend of the "Most High Priest." If Abraham, the father of faith, tithed to God, we too must follow his example as we walk by faith and not by sight. He gave a tenth of all to Melchizedek, and we too should consider giving our tenth of all to Melchizedek, who is Jesus Christ.

For it is clear that our Lord descended from Judah, and in regard to that tribe Moses said nothing about priests. [15] And what we have said is even more clear if another priest like Melchizedek appears, [16] one who has become a priest not on the basis of a regulation as to his ancestry but on the basis of the power of an indestructible life. [17] For it is declared: "You are a priest forever, in the order of Melchizedek. (Hebrews 7:14-17 NIV)

Since we have direct contact with God through our Lord Jesus Christ, we no longer need the Levites, Moses' laws, or animal sacrifices. Jesus Christ has already paid the ultimate price for all of us, and our sins have been washed away. That's why, like Abraham, we must also tithe to Melchizedek (Jesus Christ). Why? Because it pleases Him to see His children worship Him by giving a tenth of all their possessions, just as Abraham did. In return, He can only bless us abundantly. This has nothing to do with the Mosaic law, but everything to do with worshipping God and trusting Him with the first tenth of everything. As Christians, we declare ourselves spiritual heirs of Abraham. So, if we don't believe in tithing to Levites and priests because it was part of the Mosaic law and we are Christians under grace, then we should practice the tithing that existed before the law was given by Moses.

Nowhere in the New Testament does it say we should bring our tenth to the priests. You're right! But in the same

New Testament, the word "tithe" is mentioned several times. I don't understand why the New Testament needs to instruct Christians to pay tithes before they can do so. God found Abel's offering favorable.

Where was it written that a man should give offerings to God in Abel's time? God relented from destroying humankind by flooding the earth after Noah offered an offering to him. In what book did Noah read that he should give offerings to God? Likewise, Abraham was blessed after giving a tenth of everything to the High Priest. Did he read it somewhere? No! The three people I mentioned here gave offerings, and God found them favorable, not because it was written in a book or because it was a law.

They gave their offerings because of their relationship with God, and the intention of the offering was to worship Him. Therefore, rejecting this practice because it isn't explicitly instructed in the New Testament is making the Word of God obsolete because the Old Testament is the New Testament revealed. The fact that champions of faith before the law gave all sorts of offerings to God without written instruction is an indication of what is to come after Jesus, where we act not only because it's written in the Bible, but also because it's written in our hearts. "I will put my law in their minds and write it on their hearts. I will be their God, and they will be my people" (Jeremiah 31:33). Allow me to illustrate it this way. There is another saying that the Old Testament is the shadow of Christ, and the New Testament is the body of Christ. In other words, if the sun is set to noon and you look on the ground, you see the shadow of Abraham giving tithes to Melchizedek (Jesus Christ). But when you look up, you'll see Abraham (off-spring) giving tithes to Jesus Christ (Melchizedek). Both images are of the same person conducting the same act in different forms. Abraham giving tithes to Melchizedek is just a shadow for those who lived under the law, and to us, it is the physical Abraham, where the offspring that make up the body of Israel exist naturally and spiritually. That's why Jesus honored the laws by paying His tithes.

Paul said in 1 Corinthians 11:1, "And you should imitate me, just as I imitate Christ" (NLV).

I believe Paul paid his tithes because he believed Jesus paid his tithes. Why wouldn't he? Jesus Himself said in Matthew 5:17, "Do not think that I have come to abolish the Law or the Prophets; I have not come to abolish them but to fulfill them" (NIV). The key words here are "fulfill them" meaning all the laws without exception.

If Jesus came to fulfill the law, and "tithing" is part of the law, then there is no doubt He fulfilled that part too. If Paul lived his life imitating Jesus, then he must have given a tenth of all to the High Priest (Jesus). After all, he spoke at great length about tithing and Melchizedek in Hebrews Chapter 7 with conviction that, Melchizedek, described in Genesis Chapter 14, is indeed Christ the Lord.

You cannot believe the entire New Testament and pick and choose what you want to believe in the Old Testament, just to reject what you don't like in the name of "grace." That's not how Christianity works, and that's not what Christians are like. We ought to accept and believe the Bible as it is written from the first verse of Genesis to the last verse of Revelation because 2 Timothy 3:16-17 says:

"**All Scripture** is God-breathed and is useful for teaching, rebuking, correcting and training in righteousness, so that the servant of God[a] may be thoroughly equipped for every good work."

"This Melchizedek was king of Salem and priest of God Most High. He met Abraham returning from the defeat of the kings and blessed him, [2] and Abraham gave him a tenth of everything. First, the name Melchizedek means "king of righteousness"; then also, "king of Salem" means "king of peace." [3] Without father or mother, without genealogy, without beginning of days or end of life, resembling the Son of God, he remains a priest forever" (Hebrews 7:1-3 NIV).

"For it is clear that our Lord descended from Judah, and in regard to that tribe Moses said nothing about priests. [15] And what we have said is even more clear if another priest like Melchizedek appears, [16] one who has become a priest not on the basis of a regulation as to his ancestry but on the basis of the power of an indestructible life. [17] For it is declared: "You are a priest forever, in the order of Melchizedek" (Hebrews 7:14 NIV).

CHAPTER 7

TITHING IS NOT AN OBLIGATION

Is a Christian obligated to tithe? Before I answer this question, I want to be clear that my response is solely my opinion on this matter. I don't believe that paying tithe is obligatory, so the answer is no! If tithing were obligatory, people would give it with guilt and remorse. This would defeat the purpose of 2 Corinthians 9:7 where God said he loves a cheerful giver. If it were an obligation, then Malachi Chapter 3 would serve no purpose. How can you test God by doing something you don't have a say in? The test works when you do it out of your own will. God, you want me to test You? I'm in, and I can't wait to see the outcome of it. You get excited knowing that you're putting God Almighty to the test. That's the part where God enjoys a cheerful giver. You test God cheerfully and joyfully. That, my friends, activates the blessing.

So why should I tithe if I don't have to? Let's answer that, shall we?

Tithing shows that you're putting God first by giving the best of your produce. You want to tithe because God will always find your offering favorable just like Abel's offering. Your tithing will please God, and He will bless you and your descendants. When challenges arise, you and your offspring will not be destroyed as in the time of Noah. These challenges can be anything that tries to take precedence in your life, such as worries, stress, lack, and unemployment. How can tithing have such a spiritual impact on your life? As mentioned in the previous chapter; it is a form of worship. The Bible says that God dwells in worship.

"But thou *art* holy, *O thou* that inhabitest the praises of Israel" (Psalm 22:3 KJV).

When you bring your tithe into God's presence, you enter His dwelling place and can only leave blessed, just as He blessed Abraham, Isaac, and Jacob. One thing to know is that while you're in His presence, worshiping Him with a tenth of all that you have, He not only blesses you but also protects your possessions as He promised in Malachi 3:10-12:

Bring all the tithes into the storehouse, that there may be meat in my house, and prove me now herewith, saith the LORD of hosts, if I will not open you the windows of heaven, and pour you out a blessing, that there shall not be room enough to receive it. And I will rebuke the devourer for your sakes, and he shall not destroy the fruits of your ground; neither shall your vine cast her fruit before the time in the field, saith the LORD of hosts. And all nations shall call you blessed: for ye shall be a delightsome land, saith the LORD of hosts. (KJV).

"God is not a man, that he should lie; neither the son of man, that he should repent: hath he said, and shall he not do it? or hath he spoken, and shall he not make it good?" (Numbers 23:19 KJV).

Taxes vs. Tithing

Paying taxes to the government is an obligation that has existed for ages. No matter what era or type of government you want to live under, you will be subject to taxation in one way or another. Governments do not care about the conditions in which you pay your taxes; whether you pay cheerfully or complain, all they want is their share of your hard work. This system is not new. Taxation is a perverted form of legalistic tithing, whereas paying your tithe to God is no longer a law, but a willing act that can activate God's promises upon you and open the windows of heaven for you. As long as you give out of love with a cheerful heart to your God, the Creator of heaven and earth, your act of tithing becomes worship.

If anyone worships money and believes that all goods and revenue belong to them, then they are serving mammon. The Bible tells us in Matthew 6:24, "No one can serve two masters: either they will hate the one and love the other, or they will be devoted to the one and despise the other. You cannot serve both God and money."

Another benefit of tithing is that it can help you detach yourself from dependency on the world economy and instead set your dependency on God's economy. God's economy is recession and depression-proof, and investing in it will always activate abundance in times of need. You have no problem tithing to the world government in the form of taxation. A body of legislators gets together and passes tax laws that all citizens must pay in society, whether you like it or not. You work long hours, sometimes two jobs, and work hard to provide for your family. The government takes its share of your hard-earned money before you even see your paycheck. When the country experiences a recession, the same government that repeatedly takes your money is reluctant to assist you when you are in need.

Many taxpayers lost jobs, savings, and their homes during the recession in 2008, while the government bailed out big corporations and the average person was left to fend for themselves. But they paid their taxes. Why is that? Well, because where you pay the best of your produce (taxes), the world government operates under another system that we call the Babylonian system. The Babylonian system leaves you confused at the end, as God intended. "Let's go down and confuse them," He said. This system imposes taxes on the working class in exchange for promises of benefits that rarely, if ever, come true. Meanwhile, the elites in society benefit. In this system, you are obligated to pay in, no matter what. Yet, you are still under a curse, lacking every month. In this system, paying taxes is an obligation, and failure to do so may result in severe penalties, even jail time.

In the kingdom of God, this is not the case. Tithing in God's kingdom is not done under the law but under grace. You can be sure that every promise God has made regarding this subject will come to pass in your personal life, just as it has in mine. He is not a man to lie, and He is not confused.

"Your crops will be abundant, for I will guard them from insects and disease.[a] Your grapes will not fall from the vine before they are ripe," says the LORD of Heaven's Armies. 12 "Then all nations will call you blessed, for your land will be such a delight," says the LORD of Heaven's Armies" (Malachi 3:11-12 NLT).

CHAPTER 8

TO WHOM DO YOU TITHE?

Many Christians still struggle with the question of where and to whom you give your tithe. The Bible says to bring your tithes and offerings into the house of the Lord.

"Bring ye all the tithes into the storehouse, that there may be meat in mine house" (Malachi 3:10).

First, join a church near you that believes and teaches the true gospel of God and believes in tithing. As a member of that church, that's where you bring all the tithes as instructed in Malachi 3:10.

Deuteronomy 26:12-13 says, "When you have finished setting aside a **tenth of all** your produce in the third year, the year of the tithe, you shall give it to the **Levite, the foreigner, the fatherless** and **the widow**, so that they may eat in your towns and be satisfied."

Although this command is based on the Levite law, it is still relevant today. When you give to priests, foreigners, widows, and orphans, you are giving directly to God. If you have an intimate relationship with our High Priest (Jesus Christ), you should always give Him the best of your produce. God loved the world so much that He gave His best: His Son. His Son gave His life so that we could live and through Him, we have true salvation. His blood cleanses us, and by His wounds, we are healed. The least we can do is worship Him by giving a tenth of our best produce. I don't think that's asking too much as a tenth is the minimum. The maximum is one hundredth, which technically belongs to God since we are citizens of His kingdom. Because He is a merciful God full of grace, He allows us to bring Him only a tenth. Again, this is not too much to ask. Do you agree?

Let's revisit Deuteronomy 26:12. God commanded the people of Israel to give their tithes to four groups of people in the third year: the Levites, foreigners, orphans, and widows. Although we are not under the law, I want to shed light on this to show that it is not just an Old Testament law, but a spiritual law that Christians should apply when it comes to tithing. I have not heard any servant of God teach this. However, I believe it is important to explain because the Word of God will be preached in every nation. He also said that His disciples would be persecuted for His name's sake.

Let's identify who a foreigner is. We have people who are called to evangelize in different parts of the world. When they go to these places to spread the gospel of Christ, they are foreigners in those lands.

And He called the twelve together and gave them power and authority over all the demons and to heal diseases. And He sent them out to proclaim the kingdom of God and to perform healing. And He said to them, "Take nothing for your journey, neither a staff, nor a bag, nor bread, nor money; and do not even have two

*tunics apiece. "Whatever house you enter, stay there until you
leave that city. (Luke 9:1-4)*

Any evangelist sent to an unknown land to proclaim the
kingdom of God and demonstrate the gift of healing, deliverance, and soul-winning is a foreigner. A prophet who is
sent to an unknown land to deliver a word from God is also
considered a foreigner. It is important to keep in mind that
evangelization ministry is a full-time job. These individuals
are servants of the Lord who have answered the call to go
to the ends of the earth from Asia, Africa, Europe, America,
and other places, to bring you the good news and do the
work of God. If you are not a member of a church or if there
are no churches nearby and you decide to attend a service
held by an evangelist who is visiting your town, then I
believe you should bring your tithe to him or her. That is
their salary according to Deuteronomy 26:12.

Matthew 10:10 says, "Don't hesitate to accept hospitality,
because those who work deserve to be fed" (NLT).

We know that there are nations to this day that do not
allow Christians to assemble. In fact, some nations do not
have a Christian church. Although Christians are in the
minority in these places and there are no churches, they still
find a way to assemble and worship God in their homes.
So, to whom do these Christians who do not have a local
church pay their tithes? I believe they should bring their
tithes to the widows and orphans in their towns. If you
know of anyone in your community who has lost a spouse
and is struggling to make ends meet for herself and her
children since the death of the provider, as a Christian, you
should be there to support her emotionally and with your
prayers. You should feel free to assist her and her children

financially, and the best way to do this is to bring your tithe to her. This is the Christian thing to do and a way to show the nature of Christ within you, especially when you live in areas where there are no churches and where Christian assembly is forbidden.

If you know of any child or children who have lost both parents and have no one to turn to, you might not be able to meet all their needs or convince the government that you can legally take them under your wing. But what you can do is bring your tithe to them. Giving to foreigners, widows, and fatherless children is giving to God. This is not about the Old and New Testaments; it's a matter of the heart. It's about showing God's kind of love. That, my friend, is the true definition of religion. There is a reason why God instructed the Hebrews to bring their tithes to the widows and fatherless. He expects us to do the same, and He gave us the reason in the book of James.

"Pure and undefiled religion before our God and Father is this: to care for orphans and widows in their distress and to keep oneself from being polluted by the world" (James 1:27).

That is the definition of true religion, and anything else is idolatry according to God.

I believe that it's okay to do this with your tithes only if you do not have a church or if you live in a region where churches are not allowed and you worship in the comfort of your home. If you are a member of a church in your community or outside of your community, then your priority is to pay your tithes to your local church. If you do not know of any foreigners (evangelists, prophets, or apostles), widows, and fatherless in your community, then you bring your tithes to the house of the Lord (your local church). That is the salary of your spiritual leader and anyone else who works in the ministry full-time. These are the modern-day Levites. They have dedicated their time to maintaining the church and supporting the leader of the church in the mission the Lord has called them to do.

You also give your tithes to your local church because the church is set in the community to be a moral ground, to preach the Word of the kingdom of God, and to engage with the people in the community. They are aware of what is happening in the neighborhood. It is the role of the church to connect with its community and to know the foreigners, the widows, and the fatherless. Bringing your tithes to the local church helps support their needs. The church reaches out to them with any goods and products they might need.

There will always be foreigners because Jesus asks us to go into the world and make disciples of Christ. There will always be widows and the fatherless. Jesus will never forsake them, nor should we if we have the nature of Christ in us and us in Him. We are the body of Christ; therefore, we need to live out that nature and not forsake the widows and fatherless.

CHAPTER 9

TITHES IN THE NEW TESTAMENT

When debating someone who doesn't believe that we should tithe under grace, they will sometimes mention to you that it is not written in the New Testament that we should pay or don't have to pay our tithes. If the argument is that it is not written in the New Testament, then it must be that they don't read the Bible or they have been preached the wrong message because Paul mentioned it six times in Hebrews Chapter 7:4-10.

*See how great this man was to whom Abraham the patriarch gave a **tenth** of the spoils!* [5] *And those descendants of Levi who receive the priestly office have a commandment in the law to take **tithes** from the people, that is, from their brothers,[a] though these also are descended from Abraham.* [6] *But this man who does not have his descent from them received **tithes** from Abraham and blessed him who had the promises.* [7] *It is beyond dispute that the inferior is blessed by the superior.* [8] *In the one case **tithes** are received by mortal men, but in the other case, by one of whom it is testified that he lives.* [9] *One might even say that Levi himself, who receives **tithes**, paid **tithes** through Abraham,* [10] *for he was still in the loins of his ancestor when Melchizedek met him. (ESV)*

How many times does the word "tenth" or "tithe" need

to be mentioned in the New Testament before we accept that it applies to us under grace, and not just to those in the Old Testament? God's message through Paul is clear. In verse 8, Paul states that tithes are received by mortal men, specifically the Levi priests. However, in the other case, it is testified that someone lives. This someone is Jesus, the One we testify lives. Therefore, Jesus also receives our tithes now. We should not rob Him because the High Priest awaits our tithes. Just as Levi paid his tithes through Abraham because he was still in Abraham's loins when Melchizedek met him, we too pay our tithes for the same reason.

If Melchizedek had met Abraham more than once, Abraham would have given him a tenth on every occasion. Jesus, the High Priest, is alive and with us every day. This is a compelling reason to honor Him with everything, including our tithes. Although Paul does not directly instruct us to honor God with our tithes, he indirectly instructs us by emphasizing that Melchizedek, who met Abraham, is the living High Priest whom death did not conquer.

Mortal men became priests through legal requirements, without an oath. They had to offer sacrifices daily for their own sins and the sins of the people. The law appointed mortal men as high priests, but death met them all. However, Jesus, as the High Priest, has no need to offer sacrifices daily for the people. He did this once for all humanity when He died on the cross—an ultimate sacrifice. He is the word of the oath, existing before the law and coming after the law, appointing a Son who has been made perfect forever. Jesus is the only priest in the likeness of Melchizedek, the priest forever according to the order of Melchizedek. Alleluia!

This becomes even more evident when another priest arises in the likeness of Melchizedek, [16] who has become a priest, not based on a legal requirement concerning bodily descent, but by the power of an indestructible life. [17] For it is witnessed of him, "You are a priest forever, after the order of Melchizedek." [18] For on the one hand, a former commandment is set aside because of its weakness and uselessness [19] (for the law made nothing perfect); but on the other hand, a better hope is introduced, through which we draw near to God. [20] And it was not without an oath. For those who formerly became priests were made such without an oath, [21] but this one was made a priest with an oath by the one who said to him: "The Lord has sworn and will not change his mind, 'You are a priest forever.'" [22] This makes Jesus the guarantor of a better covenant. (Hebrews 7:15-22 ESV)

Paul advised us to imitate him as he imitates Jesus. His profound revelation of who Melchizedek was is meant to lead us to understand that the High Priest Abraham gave a tenth of all to is the same High Priest we have today: Jesus Christ. If Jesus is the High Priest, then we ought to give Him a tenth of all. It's that simple. There's nothing to debate. You already believe in Him. You love Him. In fact, we should love Him with all our hearts, souls, and strength. That kind of love requires giving our all to Him, including our earnings and possessions. I don't believe it's fair to say that you love God with all your heart, soul, and strength while hiding your money from Him or not trusting Him with your earnings. By the way, that's robbing God, as stated in Malachi Chapter 3. I also don't believe that loving God with all your heart, soul, and strength will prompt you to give out of guilt. Quite the contrary, that kind of love will inspire you to give cheerfully and joyfully whatever you possess. So why not imitate Paul in this case as he imitates Christ, and bring our tenth of all to the High Priest forever, Jesus Christ? With love!

CONCLUSION: FAITHFULL TITHERS

Where do I stand on this subject? I stand on the side of those who believe tithing is a biblical principle. I believe that every Christian ought to be a tither, not because a preacher says so on the altar, but because it is written, and it is the right and spiritual thing to do. When you take 10 percent of your income and bring it to the Eternal One (the Lord), it shows you trust God as the source of your income by sowing in the "economy" of His kingdom, and in return, you will reap the harvest in both the rainy days and the dry days. When I tithe, I believe that I am no longer depending on the economy of any government in this world; rather, I depend on the economy that is recession-proof and depression-proof: the divine economy.

I believe in God's promise that I will never lack; He will rebuke the devourer for my sake, and the produce of my land will not be destroyed before its time. Tithing is part of my Christian walk.

"And they overcame him by the blood of the Lamb, and by the word of their testimony; and they loved not their lives unto the death" (KJV).

Remember, this is the only time you are allowed to test God according to Malachi 3:10.

As you are about to read these testimonies, remember tithing is the only time you are allowed to test God according to the Bible, specifically Malachi 3:10.

Tithers' Testimonies

I asked some Christians who happen to be faithful tithers five questions and told them to answer however they felt like. These Christians were not aware that I was writing a book and I intended to include their testimonies in it before answering these questions. They did not know why I wanted them to share their comments and testimonies until after they had sent them to me.

1. What is tithing?
2. What does tithing represent in your life?
3. When was the first time you paid your tithe, and what made you decide to start paying it?
4. What kind of impact does tithing have on your life?
5. What would you say to people who do not believe in tithing as a biblical principle?

Sister Aline

Tithing is the act of giving 10 percent of your income. I can't quite recall when I first paid my tithe, but I believe it was after I rededicated my life to God and understood the importance of tithing. Tithing represents obedience and gratitude to God. When I give my tithe, it serves as a reminder that God has given me the strength to work. Paying my tithe has a significant impact on my spiritual and physical life. It brings me comfort knowing that I am contributing to the storehouse of the Lord. To those who don't believe in tithing as a biblical principle, I would say that we have been instructed to give our tithes from the Old Testament to the New Testament. It's a principle that can open doors in one's life. In Matthew 23:23, Jesus said that we should continue to tithe, but we should not just do it religiously. We should give with our hearts, always remembering mercy, faith, and justice.

Brother Arsene K.

A tithe is a tenth of your salary, meaning it is 10 percent of your income. In the Old Testament, the Lord commanded Israel to tithe, which means giving a tenth of their salary (Leviticus 27:30-32). Every time your salary increases, your tithe should increase by the same amount.

Not paying the tithe has negative consequences. It is said that if we neglect to pay our tithes, God Himself will bring drought, causing our efforts to produce no results. When something comes from God, no one can fix it (Haggai 1:11).

On the positive side, paying your tithes and offerings is a covenant assurance for business success, and God will bless your business with success.

What I would say to those who do not believe in tithing as a biblical principle is that although Christians have not received the same commandment in the New Testament, the Old Testament still commanded Israel to tithe. Should we be satisfied just because it is not a principle in the new covenant? The fundamental question is how we should give with the right spirit. It should be noted that managing your money is not only a responsibility but also a privilege and a pleasure. We learn in 2 Corinthians 9:7 how we are to give:

- With a specific goal, not randomly
- Voluntarily, not by force
- With joy and contentment
- In secret, not to be seen (Matthew 6:2-4)
- Honestly, not pretending to give everything while withholding part for ourselves (Acts 5:1-4)

When we give for the work of the Lord or His servants, we are giving to the Lord Jesus Christ. Let us always remember that all offerings are meant for God to bless us abundantly.

Brother Alain T

A tithe is one-tenth of our entire income. It protects our income and opens other opportunities. God spared the life of a brother involved in a car accident. He lost control of his vehicle while driving, and the car flew over the bridge and sunk in the river. Under the river, he saw a man who said to him, "Come out and go pay your tithe that you had set aside." This was the money he earned prior to the accident.

It is important for us to pay our tithes because it opens the floodgates of heaven in our favor. God bless!

Sister Christine M

Tithes are the first one-tenth of my revenue. Each time I pay my tithes regularly, I see a lot of very good doors open to me (the blessings of God). For those who do not believe in tithing or pay their tithes sparingly, I would say you are making a mistake. Giving is receiving. How much more if you give to God and support His work? Tithing brings material and non-material blessings. God bless.

Brother Mansour

A tithe is a tenth of our income that we give to the church of God. Malachi taught the importance of tithing and the blessings that come from obeying this law. For me, paying tithes is a sign of our faith in Jesus Christ. If we trust in Him, we will be strengthened, guided, and supported in our lives. The payment of tithes is a sacred right. Prosperity, in its simplest form, means that a person sows a seed and later reaps the returns. Those who do not pay tithes become poorer because they have nothing to harvest; they do not attract blessings in their lives.

Brother Jean J. B.

For me, a tithe is the part that we give to God after receiving payment. Tithing has a multiplier effect on my life; it protects my activities. Each time I tithe, it comes back to me double or other opportunities are made available to me. I would tell those who do not believe in tithing as a biblical principle to be incredibly careful about that. Even the Devil respects and knows very well the benefits we get from tithing. That is why sometimes we lack the will to give and find it difficult to respect this principle. Generally, it happens that we plan in advance to give the tithe once rewarded for our work, but just when we get paid, we forget to give the tithe and spend the money on other things. All that, for me, is a trap of the Devil because he knows very well the power of tithing.

Sister Tanya N

For me, tithing is a percentage of all my income that I give to God as a way of thanking Him. Tithing serves as a reminder that God is the source of all my income and is the priority in everything I have. I have so many testimonies. When I don't tithe, I feel as if everything is blocked. The first job I had, I gave God my entire pay (a tithe of 100 percent of my income) for the first year, and I experienced inexplicable favor during my seven years at Vodacom (a Telephone Company in the Democratic Republic of Congo) until I became self-employed. To people who do not believe in tithing as a biblical principle, I would say, may God be merciful to them and may the Holy Spirit illuminate their hearts.

My second testimony: God is good! As I was getting the rent money for January 2024, I only had 200 U.S. dollars. In our house, we usually pay rent in advance for the month. As I was getting this money, I realized I was behind in my tithing for November and December. I had been paying 100 dollars toward my tithes for some time. Now, with 200 dollars in my hand, I started thinking. I hadn't paid my rent yet, and I was two months behind on my tithes. What should I do? I said to myself, "No, I can't cheat God. If I take my tithe offering and add it to my rent money, and if my rent money is still not enough, who will come to bail me out? But if I pay my tithes and don't have enough for rent, God will come through for me." I told myself, "I don't want to start the year 2024 owing God tithes and end up in problems later. I refuse to do that." I took this money and paid my tithes through my App. Shortly after I sent my tithes from my App on my phone, a brother came to my house to visit. He said, "I have a small amount of money I wanted to give you." He pulled the money out of his pocket. Can you guess how much it was? Two hundred dollars. When I saw it, I said to myself, "Oh God!"

Dr. Serge K. M.

It is a mark of gratitude to the Lord for life, His grace, and His infinite goodness to devote a tenth of our earnings or income (in kind or cash) to Him. Tithing serves as a constant reminder of my complete dependence on the Lord. Each time I dedicate a tenth of my income to Him, I acknowledge that everything I am and possess comes from Him. Tithing centers my life on the glory of God and cultivates gratitude, humility, and a sense of security in belonging to Him. I learned this principle in high school and continued to practice it even when studying abroad with a minimal scholarship. Despite setbacks and challenges, my scholarship was never interrupted, which I consider exceptional and miraculous. I lived for years with a constant fear of my student career collapsing or receiving news about the termination of my scholarship, but that never happened. It's a miracle that will remain with me for the rest of my life.

Brother Arsene B.

A tithe is an obligatory investment that I must set aside to support my Christian community or others. Knowing that I receive returns by giving, I believe that God makes me a financial deposit through which others can receive their shares. I believe that everything I have been able to achieve so far is because God is the primary investor and partner in all my life projects, and His investment always goes up to 10 percent.

Sister Eminence

A tithe represents a tenth of all your wages. God has always provided for me financially and in every other aspect of my life. As a testimony, even when I did not have a job, God took care of me and my family. I do not judge those who don't believe in tithing as a biblical principle because I understand that they may not be convinced. For this reason, I pray that the Holy Spirit will work in their hearts and bring them understanding.

Brother Collins Bahini

Tithing is giving a tenth of our income, and the practice was first demonstrated by Abraham in Genesis 14:17-20. Tithing serves as a spiritual connection between God and us. In fact, tithing provides not only spiritual protection but also material protection. Tithing serves to close the doors to the devourer as stated in Malachi 3:10.

Tithing has helped me avoid overdrawing my bank account. It has also protected me against theft. One day, I left my money in an envelope, and typically, when an envelope is empty, I tear it up and throw it away. But this time, I did not tear or discard the envelope. Later, as I was going through my papers, the Spirit of God prompted me to look inside the envelope. To my surprise, the money was still there.

For those who don't believe that tithing is a biblical principle, I say, it is well written, and we cannot take what gives us pleasure and leave others. Tithing is undeniably rooted in the Bible, and those who reject it should carefully examine God's teachings. These falsehoods are the Devil's tactics to discourage our obedience to the Word of God (Joshua 1:8).

Sister Gisele M.

I have so many testimonies about the faithfulness of God through the tithing principle. He never lies. What he says in Malachi 3:9-12, He certainly accomplishes. The Lord multiplied what I had a hundredfold because I was faithful with my tithes. I am what I am today thanks to the tithing principle. The statement "Thus, saith the Lord" in the Bible are fulfilled in my life in an incredible and unexpected way. Yes, the Lord is too good and faithful. He always cares for me, I hardly get sick, he gives me wisdom, intelligence, and strategies on how to excel and breakthrough in my business.

I started my small business 13 years ago with 80 dollars

as a capital and, today I have thousands of dollars in my account. I have travelled to many countries in Africa, Asia and Europe and, the Lord God still continue to open doors for me in every way, because I am faithful with my tithe, and I believe in His promises. As I said here, I have many testimonies such as this. Our God is wonderful, full of goodness. Let us remain confident in God, he always acts, and he always fulfils his promises. May the fear of the Lord and the ardent desire to serve him always be our part.

I hope that you are inspired by these testimonies of fellow Christians who have unequivocally understood and believed that, paying their tithes is a Biblical principle. Now that you have read their testimonies, I hope you too will take a leap of faith and bring your tithes and offerings to the treasure house, not with a heart of guilt, but with a heart of worship to God as a citizen of the kingdom. God's kingdom. This leap of faith will be the ultimate act of faith for you to test God, so He can act upon his Word as it is written in Malachi 3, so you can experience it for yourself if he will not "throw open the floodgates of heaven and pour out so much blessing that there will not be room enough to store it and, prevent pests from devouring your crops, and the vines in your fields will not drop their fruit before it is ripe."

I'd like to conclude this book by reiterating what the Lord himself says "Return to me, and I will return to you." In my definition of the word "return" there's restoration, healing (return to wholeness) and there is abundance. It also means that you are going the wrong way. If you are going the wrong way, then you need to stop and take a 180-degree turn. "Return" means, going back to the starting point. If you return, then you now standing before Holiness. When he is asking us to return to him, he is extending his hand to us so we can return to where it all started in Genesis 1. To a better place where there is no dire (Depression, Inflation, Recession and Emptiness), a safe environment, and a place of abundance. The Biblical principle of tithing and offerings is one of the keys that take us back into God's abundance. That is why he used this key to remind us in Malachi 3, to return to him. So, if you decide to make a vow to God today, that from now on I am returning to you with my tithes, and if you decide to make your tithes part of your act of loving the Lord your God with all your heart, and with all your soul, and with all your mind, and with all your strength, as he instructed us, then I truly believe that you are beginning the process of healing, restoration, and abundance and, your house will become a treasure house.

Trust God and test him on this. Believe me. This Biblical principle worked then, and it still works now. It will work in your favor too in Jesus Christ name.

TEACHINGS RECOMMENDATION

Now that you have decided to take that leap of faith and become a faithful tither, I want to encourage you to find a local church in your area that believes and teaches this Biblical principle. If you don't have a local church in your area, but you want to grow spiritually in your walk with Jesus Christ, then allow me to recommend to you the teaching of four of the generals of God in the body of Christ, Dr. Mensah Otabil, Dr. Myles Monroe, Dr. Frederick Price Sr. and Kenneth Hagin. You can find their teaching on YouTube, or you can buy their books anywhere Christian books are sold. The reason I am recommending these four men of God, is because they have earned their stripes and served God with dignity and honor. Furthermore, they have the gift of teaching in a way that anyone at any spiritual level could comprehend.

Although three of the four servants have gone to be with the Lord, their teachings remain relevant to this day, and it testifies of their relationship with God. I am certain that their teachings will help you grow spiritually, because it is written; "Heaven and earth will pass away, but my words will never pass away." (Matthew 24:35). They're pastor, speaker, and leadership expert in their own right, known for their impactful teachings on faith, healing, kingdom principles, leadership and social issues. They are known for their dynamic preaching style and impactful teachings on faith, leadership, and personal development. They have impacted and influenced the world through their teachings. and I'd like to believe "they have fought the good fight; they have finished the race and they have kept the faith." They are the true role models in the body of Christ. That's why I'm recommending their teachings.

Some key aspects of their teachings that I and many Christians often admire:

1. **Biblical Foundation:** Teachings of these four men of God are firmly rooted in scripture, and they often provide in-depth exegesis and application of biblical principles to everyday life. They emphasize the importance of understanding and applying God's Word in all areas of life.

2. **Leadership Development:** Dr. Monroe and Dr. Otabil are known for their emphasis on leadership development and excellence. They teach that every individual has the potential to become a leader and encourage people to cultivate their leadership skills for personal and organizational success.

3. **Faith and Empowerment:** Dr. Myles Monroe, Dr. Price and Dr. Hagin messages often focus on faith, healing, empowerment, and personal growth. They challenge believers to step out in faith, pursue their dreams, and overcome obstacles with confidence and determination.

4. **Social Relevance:** Dr. Mensa Otabil, Dr. Myles Monroe and Dr. Frederick Price address a wide range of social and cultural issues in their teachings, providing biblical perspectives on topics such as marriage, family, finances, and social justice. They seek to make the timeless

truths of scripture relevant to contemporary challenges faced by individuals and societies.

5. **Positive Impact:** The ministries of these four generals have had a significant impact both locally and globally, inspiring millions of people to live with purpose, integrity, and excellence. Their teachings have helped individuals strengthen their faith, improve their relationships, and make a positive difference in their communities.

I hope you'll take time to listen to these men of God and be inspired and influenced by their teachings with discernment, comparing them with the principles found in scripture and seeking guidance from the Holy Spirit. I also pray that you find a local church near you and make it your church and get surrounded with trusted spiritual mentors or advisors who will help you grow in your Christian's journey.

God bless you in Jesus Christ our Savior and Lord!

9 798893 833997